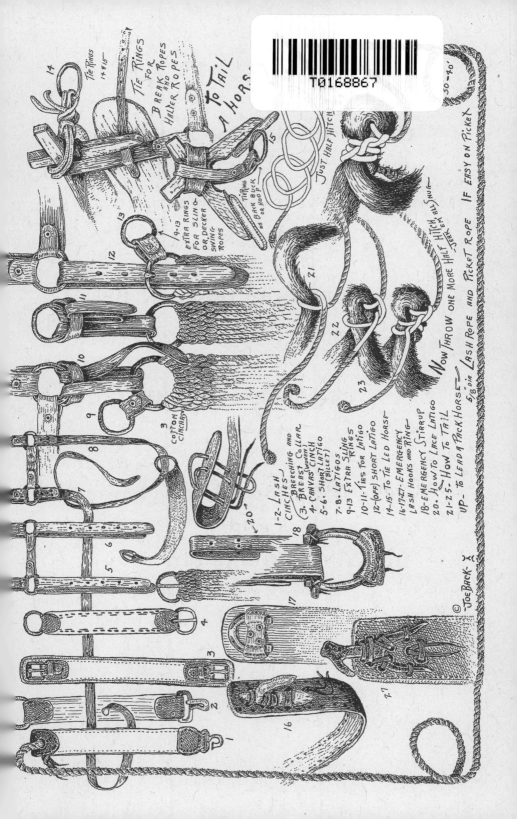

Other Books By Joe Back

Mooching Moose and Mumbling Men

by Joe Back

The Model T and the Lazy Board

by Joe Back, illustrated by Mary Back

The Sucker's Teeth

by Joe Back

The Old Guide Remembers
and
the Young Guide Finds Out

by Joe Back, with Vic Lemmon

HORSES, HITCHES & ROCKY TRAILS

JOE BACK

BOWER HOUSE

DENVER

BowerHouseBooks.com

Illustrations by Joe Back
Cover Design by Margaret McCullough

Printed in Canada

Library of Congress Catalog Card No. 59-11063
ISBN 978-1-55566-477-0

TO ALL PACKERS—
PAST, PRESENT, AND FUTURE

FOREWORD

Interest, enjoyment, and enthusiasm come naturally when we listen to, or watch, a true craftsman in his field. Joe Back lets us do both in this book, and he does it in the language of the trail. His clear word pictures could come only from the man who has thrown every hitch, and in the dark, at that. Joe's ability makes each horse live, almost move; even the final knot on a wintry pack makes one's hands cold. This knack will make collectors' items of the copies of this edition.

I am humbly proud to write these few lines for my good friends Joe and Mary Back. Western Forest Rangers, who in their work pack and use the horses and mules along the rugged rocky backbone of our nation, have a kinship with Joe. It is an area of wind-deformed timberline trees; wild water; flashing trout; big-game heads on the hoof; and today's mountain men packing the trails. Joe's home range starts where wheeled travel stops. To haul loads successfully in this country and not hurt your animals takes know-how. Much of the know-how you now have in your hands has never been written down before. Rangers, outfitters, and many so-called dudes will use this handbook, and be thankful every day they have it on the trail. I am gratified to see this part of the lore and knowledge of man so engagingly recorded for those who come after us.

When you fry up those fine fresh eggs with your breakfast ham, thirty miles from the last tire track, the craftsmanship Joe gives us here is what made it possible for them to make the trip in one piece.

Joe is talking about mountains, not hills; where the eagle's scream comes from a big white-headed bird with inch and a half talons that is circling just above you, not from the paymaster's window; where "you lay down and look up twice" to see the notch in the rim that you must pass through; where your horse "sticks his tail in the ground" and slides to the bottom; where he claws like a cat up ledge after ledge, each one about level with his eyes when he starts to scramble. Those that heed Joe's advice can make such trips comfortably and not sore-back an animal.

When you finish this trip with Joe and have lingered over the drawings till you're satisfied, pick up a rope and do some practicing. The appeal is universal, be you ranger, professional packer, dude, or one of us who for some reason must do his packing right at home. When you can, come over and see us and Tie Your Own Diamond.

PAT MURRAY
Forest Supervisor
Shoshone National Forest
Cody, Wyoming

CONTENTS

Foreword, by *Pat Murray*   6

Introduction   11

What Makes a Camp Good?   13

Packing Horses from Away Back   23

Getting Along with a Pack Horse   33

This Is the Gear   52

Pack Saddles   57

Equipment   60

Balancing the Load   62

Packing Up Right   65

Finishing Hitches and Final Ties   79

Rope Shortage—Repairs and Makeshifts   92

On the Trail   96

Making Camp   105

Getting Along with the Wilderness   108

This Is the End   113

Appendix   116

ILLUSTRATIONS

Miscellaneous details	*endpapers*
A good camp	*frontispiece*
Details of a good camp	14
We had all our outfit and meat and were headed out	21
Comparative anatomy	24
Trails where eagles lost their way	26
Bridger and Cortez move on	28
Genuine squaw hitch	31
Sometimes a small insurrection turns up	34
Apprentice on way to kindergarten	38
Introduction to teacher	39
Tangled up with teacher	39
Graduated	40
Teacher's pet	41
To picket a shod horse by halter . . .	42
To hold a horse	43
Tieing up a hind leg	44
Leg up and no see	46
The Running W	47
Strait jacket	49
There's lots of gentle mules	50
This is the gear	53
Pack saddles	58
Balance your saddle	63
Panniers	69
Metal panniers	70
Meat packing	71
Elk horns	72
Basket and barrel hitches	73
Slings	74
Some ways to do it	75

To sling and pack a riding saddle 78

The long and short of it 80

Diamond hitch 84

Double diamond hitch 85

Double diamond hitch 86

One man diamond 87

Never sweat diamond hitch 88

Box hitch 89

To cross a bridge 91

A rope hackamore 94

Tailing up 97

Meat horses tailed 98

Tied wrong and in trouble 99

Let 'em pick their own way 99

Suicide type packer—tied to saddle horn 100

Riding a wring-tail—no time to roll a smoke 100

Rope happy gent in a jam 102

Tug of war, and no holds barred 106

If you can't pack it out, don't kill it 109

So long pardner . . . when you come to the end of your rope . . . 114

Tie a knot in it and hang on! 115

INTRODUCTION

It's been many years, scars, and ropeburns since I first saw the Rockies and fell in love with them. When you're young, love at first sight is a natural thing, but I guess I never grew up! This romance is still going on.

To explore the heart of these hills, it was necessary to find a way to finance the courtship. If you want to find out some of the devious ways it took me to do it, my friend, you'll have to be a reckless gambler, and read the rest of this love letter.

When you are lucky enough to find yourself about to explore the mysteries and joys of those hazy peaks and rushing rivers, you ask one of the squint-eyed, wrinkled-up old packers if he likes his snorty, rope-jerkin' trade. He'll rub his whiskers and clink his spurs on a rock, and gaze off at that clump of golden aspen nestled high up in a spruce-fringed canyon on the mountainside.

He'll say that there is a lot of better-paying jobs, but guiding and packing is all he knows.

Pardner, he's a rim-rocked old liar. Look at him close, he's got that lovesick mountain glitter in his shifty eye. He'd blush and cuss if he knew you'd found he was in love with the same old pine-covered, snow-capped girl you'd fallen for!

Don't think I invented any of these tangled-up conglomerations of wood, leather, rope, and metal thing-a-ma-jigs herein described in my crude way. Like the other lovesick idiots I have enjoyed working with, I may have adapted and changed some of the horse and mule jewelry with which the courtship was, and still is, carried on. I am not old enough yet (and I was born in the nineteenth century), to have met up with the bird who invented any of the hitches and ties you'll find in the rest of this deal. I'll have to admit, though, that some of the bow-legged confidence men I know *claim they have.* I have learned all these love knots and hairy hitches from other men. For a lot of rocky miles and weathered years I have practiced this little-known trade. If what I have put down here is of some value and interest to you, I will have but passed on what was passed to me. There've been adaptations and whimsical changes, and maybe fancied improvement, but mainly it's what has been used from the shadowy long gone procession of men and pack animals.

So right now I want to thank the many friends, packers, employers, and other hands I have known and worked with, who have egged on this romance with hints, helps, and general onery bits of friendly tips.

It is much easier to put an A-1 pack on an animal than it is to draw the way it's done, and the unbelievers who don't agree with this declaration can get the paper and pencils gratis from yours truly. It's even harder to do the writing, and get everything put together to make sense. In the preparation of this book I am especially indebted to my good friends Mr. Pat Murray, Dr. Olaus Murie, and Mr. Maurice Frink, for their many helpful suggestions and technical advice. And I want to thank my dear wife, Mary, without whose help, encouragement, and criticism, this diamond-encrusted venture would never have been.

Pardner, I hope you like this book.

JOE BACK
Dubois, Wyoming

WHAT MAKES A GOOD CAMP GOOD?

A few years ago another guide and I were hazing a pack string up a steep Wyoming trail. When we broke out into a high grassy valley, there was a nifty looking, well set up hunting camp, nestled under a beautiful stand of lodgepole timber. The cook tent was close to the creek and the cook was peeling spuds. We let our pack horses rest a minute and rode over to palaver with him.

While shooting the breeze I idly noticed that some of the sleeping tents and also the cook tent had neat compact propane stoves, with the necessary shiny tanks attached nearby. Festoons of wire were strung from tent to tent. There was electric bulbs around, and a small gas engine generator lurked under a canvas shelter nearby. I noticed my pardner peering around with a furtive and dazed expression on his leathery mug.

After a cup or two of coffee with the friendly cook, we rounded up our grazing pack string and lined up the trail. When we got to our own camp six or eight miles farther up the country, we unpacked our horses, took care of our gear, belled and turned loose our string. I cut wood and started a supper fire in the cook tent while my pardner picketed a couple of night horses.

This gent was an old time guide who usually could talk your leg off. When he showed up and helped cook, he had a silly grin around his cigarette and only mumbled. We started in on our grub, ate, and cleaned up, and still no gab in answer to my cracks and comments designed to dig out his beliefs, beefs, or whatever. After a lot of cigarettes and a quart of coffee, we turned into our bedrolls and then it started.

"Didja see them lights?" says Slim.

"Sure I did," I says.

"Well, by hell, didja see them stoves and them shiny little tanks?" grunts Slim through his blankets.

"Couldn't help but see all that," says I.

"Well, dammit it all, doncha remember we used to camp in that same park by that timber a few years back? We even built that pole corral they're using, remember?" Slim reared up in bed now and he must have

13

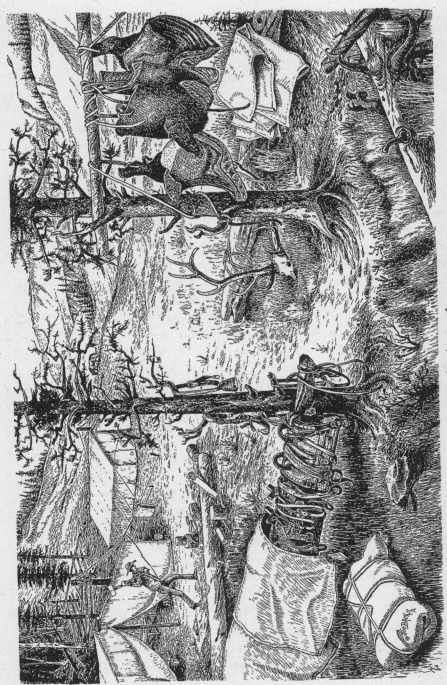

Details of a good camp.

glared at me. "One of the best camps we ever used. Good grass all around, good water, lots of wood, and fine shelter."

"That's right," I tell him.

"Well, by hell, then." Slim gets out of bed and puts another stick or two of wood in the stove. He even lights up a gas lantern, which is a godsend if ever I saw one. Then he sets down on his scrambled up bed and starts in on me right. "I'll be dagoned if I knowed you are as dumb as you seem to be. Why did I never find it out before!" Slim is really burned now and I think he must be weedy or mebbe the hills has finally got him.

"Look, stoop," says Slim behind another cigarette and gulping more coffee, grounds and all, "if you think we're going to help that Jonesy outfit, you're going to do it all by your lonesome!"

That last crack made me sure Slim had loose cinchas with a heavy top pack loaded with nitro bucking through slide rock. I reached a hand out, being closer to the stove than this nutty packer, and got hold of a good husky stick of wood, not-to-be-put-on-the-fire. All this was not lost on the worked up old rope-jerker.

He had to grin, and then he cools off and really gets to going. He's got something all right, but my mind's not with him yet. I'm thinking of those two elk we are after for our own winter meat. We'd run our camp all fall, had good luck, our hunters had all got their game and gone home, and here we were to get our own meat, pull camp, and go on down to the ranch in the valley.

Slim won't leave me be. He's really wound up now, with a glint back in his flinty gray eyes. "I didn't see *all* that outfit had, but I was sure looking past that hump in my beak, which I'm dead sure you wasn't yours! Here it is, late in the season, snow hasn't hit us yet, just a skift or two made good trackin' snow a time or two; now it's bound to come, mebbe hit us hard. You know yourself the elk have started migratin' this way, tricklin' down into the Hole. Just startin', you might say. They wasn't born yesterday (looks like you was)," he says, "neither was they born the day before. You know dern well that's a sign the big snow's a-comin' and mebbe quick. Course we gotta get our own meat in the next day or two and pull outa here. But them people down there," he jerks a bony thumb, "you can see they just got camp set up. It wasn't there a couple days ago when we took our last hunters down.

"We didn't see their guides or their hunters, only the cook. They're probably above camp, trying to get onto some game. But I seen, and you

15

musta seen, the extra horses hobblin' along just below the crick, and didn't hear a bell, mindja! So, smart guy, they just come up now, didn't they? Well, that's that." He leers around his droopy Bull Durham. "No wood stoves, camped in the best timber, probly nothin' but that electric light plant for light, must have gasoline for their light gadget. I betcha they ain't even got a gasoline lantern, ner nary a candle. Didja see where they pounded in their boughten tent stakes with a rock? Huh, forgot to bring an axe. I'll betcha they can't bury their garbage. Probly forgot a shovel, cause I see they didn't try to pole and bank their tent walls.

"Nary a sign of grain for the ponies *and* I betcha no stock salt to help hold 'em'. Yeah, yeah, course it ain't nonna my business, mebbe; mindja, just mebbe!

"You noticed them pack saddles thrown down under that tree? Blankets caked up, all a mess, that pile uh halters and packropes all jumbled up and slung on them snags by that ol corral? Yes, that's right, mebbe they wuz in a hurry and will clean up the deal when they come in. Now here's what I'm gittin' at." Slim rolls a cigarette, the bag's about empty now. "Them new tents. OK, they was set up good and tight, I'll grant ye that. Now the gas stoves, camped in a good dry pole patch, best wood. Electric light plant. Yeah, it's *their* outfit, OK, OK. No sign of oats for horses. No salt, I betcha. *Now* I'll let yuh have it, smarty.

"Comes a helluva storm, snows up, gets warm, crusts. Snows again, warms up, crusts. Them guys'll run out of gas in them tanks, takes a lotta gasoline in that light plant, mebbe no candles or lamps to fall back on, no wood stoves. I'll betcha on this—no oats. Comes a big shutdown storm, horses get weak counta snow too crusty to paw down for feed. All that Jonesy layout points to man comfort, no horse comfort, no practical look-ahead. No oats! No axe! Oh hell!"

All this hullabaloo got me roused up. I put my stick of stovewood in the fire and got up to close the tent flaps. It was spittin' snow when I stuck my nose out in the dark. I could hear our horse bells down in the grassy creek bottom below camp. Boy, was I glad we'd packed in a good bunch of grain. One of the horses on a picket log back of camp whinnied, and was answered by a pal down on the crick. Going to hit us all right. Slim can be wrong, and he blamed his hunch on the way the elk was movin', but his arthritis knew a storm was comin'.

When I turned around, Slim got up off his bedroll and went to look outside too. His long bony nose twitching and him shivering in his long underwear made me make a crack about a skinny moose we'd seen. Slim got back in his bedroll and grunted, "Homely and onery as you are, you got no room to insult your betters!"

I shut the stove off and turned out our gas lamp. Boy, I'm glad we always banked and poled up our tents. This cook tent we had was sure snug. Slim had one more crack. "Yeah, and did you see that flimsy ol' deadwood picket pin they had drove? We passed it just after we left their camp. Well, by hell." The last thing I heard, before the snores started, was snow sifting in colder pellets against the tent walls.

Next morning she was really coming down, warm for this time of year, but boy you could see this was going to pile up. A few moving objects could barely be seen through the floury mist of falling snow. A slight breeze cleared up a timbered ridge across the creek, and you could dimly see a line of elk coming down a game trail in the gathering morning light. The storm had started the elk migrating toward their winter range below. More elk sounds could be heard closer to camp.

Well, Slim and I got a couple of dry cow elk easy enough. Packed 'em in and settled down to cleaning up our camp, stacking poles, and packing up our outfit. We took our time and figured we'd pull out in a couple more days or so and call it good till next year. Our horses were good camp horses and big and stout. No horse hunting. We'd throw a couple big baits of oats into the ponies every day. No trouble.

This storm was a lulu. After a couple more days, we'd taken everything down and packed and mantied up our whole outfit, except our cook tent which we were using till last. Our eight quarters of elk were frozen hard and ready to take out. The next day we wrangled early, and after breakfast had most of our horses packed. We were just folding up our cook tent to put on top of the last pack horse, when we heard a holler along the trail. We could barely see a man stumbling towards us in the falling snow. He made heavy weather as we'd had about eighteen inches of snow down already, heavy and soggy.

Slim looked over the withers of the horse we had ready to throw the last pack on. The horses were snorting as they stared at the tired-out man pushing weakly through the soggy snow, but Slim snorted the loudest. I walked over and helped him get to a fire we still had going against a big rock. He sat down on a picket log and nearly fell off. Slim came and poured some coffee out of an old tin can we had propped up as a stirrup cup, you might say. This guy dang near needed help to get this coffee up to his mouth.

17

Slim looked over at me with a sour, knowing, told-you-so look, and says, "Say, young feller, ain't you the feller who wrangled horses last summer on the PDQ summer trips? Thought I'd seen you before."

The young fellow give us the whole story, while we was getting him fixed up. We unpacked a horse and got some canned beans and meat warmed up. Slim and me dug into our war bags, and made this bird take off his soaked and half freezing pants and underwear. He had fancy high-heeled boots on that were dang near impossible to yank off. We had an extra pair of packs and wool socks that fit him, so we got him warmed and fed up till he could talk without shaking to pieces.

He had went to work with a new outfit that had bought an old ranch that spring down the valley towards town. His boss had plenty of money and liked comfort, and how. That was the outfit we'd went past coming back to camp. This bird who owned the outfit had another young feller working for him and about four friends of his from some city who he was treating to a deluxe hunting trip.

Well, I'll be dad-burned if it didn't come out just like Slim said—he don't need a glass ball, just his jumped-on old hat. The first night it snowed was the night their hard luck caught up with them.

Everything bore out what this young fellow said about his boss: a good guy to work for, but one of these exuberant hurry-up boys. "Let's get to going, ain't them mountains beautiful! I can't wait to get camp set up and show these old friends of mine what a *real* camp is. None of these old hillbilly hardships for me. Fellows, we're going to do this up brown. The bull elk we'll get up there will show people you don't have to go through a lot of hardships to hunt in these hills. This is the *Modern Age,* and we are going to have a *De Luxe Outfit!*"

No oats, of course. "This weather'll hold, and boys, look at all that good grass!"

Mebbe all that happened was funny afterwards, but it couldn't have been very humorous that night.

Seems like after the two young wranglers, the cook, the boss, and his friends from the city had got to the spot and unpacked their string, they had all pitched in and had set up the camp. The new stoves had directions on how to connect tanks and set up ready to go—the light plant, same way. Everything worked fine. Well, till the storm hit. The boss was tickled at the way things were going. His friends got a big buck deer first morning. A big happy camp, all the comforts of home, and "Boys, ain't it great to

18

be in the last wilderness plumb full of game, and did you ever dream of such golden days? Those quaking aspen groves over there with those peaks behind them to show 'em off is prettier than any artist could ever paint!"

I have been ramming over these mountains for a long time. Slim is only a couple years older than me and has followed the same sort of life. We both have got ourselves into a lot of crazy jackpots, but we usually got out of them without too much agony except that mental kick-yourself which is worse than physical aches and pains. Slim and I both have some modern conveniences at home, they're sure handy and save a lot of trouble. I'm just writing here what can happen to you if you get *too* civilized. The lack of two or three cave men tools and a few simple precautions can sometimes bring modern men to disaster and even death.

Seems like it all happened at once just like a bad dream.

The night it stormed everybody was out hunting. When they got into camp after dark, the cook was cussing. His propane stove had no gas, and when he unhooked a tank off a heating stove in a sleeping tent, it wouldn't fit his stove. He tried to cook on one of those little heating stoves, and was at it when the light generator went off. About this time the crowd rode in. It was snowing pretty good now and plumb dark. The boss says, "I'll fix that," so he goes over to a close clump of spruce to find the gasoline can for the light generator. In the snow-covered brush he kicked around to find the five-gallon can. He lit a match to help see better. If it hadn't been for the snow, he'd have lost more than that old-mountain-man beard he'd cultivated all summer. His yells brought everybody over to see who a bear had killed, but only found an empty five-gallon can old Singed Whiskers had accidentally knocked over in the snowy dark. Then the hungry bunch went back to the cook tent and found a couple weak flashlights. When one of them lit a gas stove in one of the little tents, it burned awhile and went out. All the others must of had leaky connections, because none of them had fuel.

No axe. They'd even forgotten their hunting hatchets when they hurried up to leave the ranch for the trip. One of the boys knew about picketing his horse to a loose log; but with no axe or saw to trim a deadfall, had resorted to pounding in a dead tree-limb with a rock, for his night-horse. They weren't so happy now. They went to kicking around in the snow for dead branches and pulling squaw wood off the lodgepole trees back of camp to build up a fire in front of the cook tent. Then the weak flashlight batteries give out. About this time one of the wranglers and the cook, who

19

were together dragging down a hefty little dead tree toward the cook tent, had the scare of their lives. Something big and black ran past them and down the creek it went. A horse gave a loud roaring snort. There was a popping crack, and pounding feet drummed off dimly in the heavier falling snow. There were some distant rumbles and startled whinnies and busted limbs, telling of the departing picket horse and his homesick cronies. Must have been a scavenging bear who livened up the works.

Well, the can openers got hell that night, and most everybody thought to hell with it and fumbled into their sleeping bags. The boss had the cook cinch up a nice piece of bacon rind on his manly chin before everything settled down to a muttering quiet for the night.

It sure must have been a picture next morning in that camp. During the night one of the imported tent poles busted in the middle, owing to being too weak to resist the pressure of the snow and wet canvas and tent pegs. And a big dead lodgepole fell over and crashed close to another tent. No one was hurt, but the hunters must have lost a few years of going to be "good old men." Me, I always look at tree conditions before I pitch any kind of camp. Deadfalls or blowdowns will sure put the fear into humans.

The two wranglers in with the cook had done all right. They had a big fire going out in front and everyone had grub. Soaked clothing and bruised feelings everybody had in common.

The boys took out in the deepening snow to look for horses. Their camp was about twenty-six miles travel above their ranch. They soon figured that the whole bunch had migrated along with the traveling elk that were showing up along the timbered ridges. The two wranglers found sign of their horse bunch, all right, and especially of the one dragging the busted-off picket pin. They hoped they'd find him snagged up in the timber with that anchor, but nothing stopped him. He traveled right along according to the tracks. They had to conclude he was an old skid horse for sure. They came across no other camps of hunters, so finally went back towards camp and got there before night, more dead than alive. The snow was piling up, and thicker falling. A couple of the Daniel Boones from the big city had went up on the ridge above camp and had killed a couple of old bull elk, so all the crew had gone back with the boys to try to drag them down towards camp.

Well, there was one thing and another, including a strange foot hunter who wandered into camp half froze and lost, and the boss showing signs of appendix or liver or something besides a blistered chin. The cook told

We had all our outfit and meat and were headed out.

the boss about us and what we'd said about our camp. So this boy had finally come up to see what could be done.

You wouldn't know it from that homely wrinkled up mug of Slim's, that he is trying to hide a heart as big as a moose's paunch. Them growls and jeers is the camouflage he uses, he figures will help out his bluff. So after we heard about the deal, we double-packed one horse, put the kid on the worked over old army pack saddle, on another, and took off down toward his camp. At least we had all our meat and outfit and were headed out. Those guys were glad to see us, and how! We unloaded our stoves and pipe, a saw, an axe or two, a shovel, some gasoline and gas lamps, and most of our oats. We put a couple of the hunters and the boss (who was pretty sick) on some of our horses, using their saddles, to go on in. One wrangler went with us to find his horses and to come back to camp with them. He had some trouble with them, and we helped him get them up the trail. We made a trip back and helped them out. That outfit finally got everything out of the mountains, and nobody the worse for it.

Atomic Age or not, there is a lot of ancient skills and tools that will always be needed. Survival even in this modern age many times will depend on just a few essentials and very simple ones at that. I reckon the moral for this tale could be that no matter how modern you are, just take a few Stone Age precautions.

That yarn is how this book came to be written. I know something about those old skills of survival, I thought. And I can draw pretty fair. I've never seen or heard of a book devoted mainly to packing the horse, only a few short articles, most of them with illustrations from photographs. While there has been men in this pack horse deal longer, and plenty of them before I was born, they haven't written about it. These birds are too busy packing, or they've left it and gone into something else. Mebbe they think it's so simple, why waste your time.

I'm simple enough to believe it might interest somebody else. It might even help them in a tight spot. I've put in a good many years at packing, and I'm still a pessimistic optimist.

PACKING HORSES FROM AWAY BACK

Better men than I have wrote many paper factories' output about "the man on the horse." But they are the Don Quixote type. Being of a more plebeian nature and with a less chivalrous character, I am going to stick to the Sancho Panza type of writing, about "the load on the horse." And since I'm talking about Stone Age skills, I'm going to go way back.

There has been many discussions about the wheel being invented before the horse—first, that is. I wasn't present at the birth of the wheel, but I would bet a dollar to a packsaddle that our friend the horse was up on a hill watching that first tinker figure out the wheel.

The wheel needed the horse. The horse or any animal can pull more than he can carry on his back. But the horse can go more places carrying things than pulling them. There are times when it is logical to pack the wheels or other gear upon the pony to where the wheeled outfit can again be used. The first two-legged gent who figured out how to enslave the four-legged one must have had a lot of ambition and was trying to get out of work. Here was a great source of unused power. People now use in machines power transmission—the horse who first kicked a man had that figured out. This here power ejection on airplanes must have been derived from the man who got bucked off, the first time was long ago. Power steering was gotten from a hard-mouthed horse. I've even known some hydramatic packers, you know, shiftless.

No one will even know whether the horse was first rode, packed, or hooked onto some contrivance to pull it. The bird who says he knows is a pretty old man, and I kind of wonder if he invented how to stray a mite from the truth. If he knows the horse was rode before he was packed he has got more information and gullibility, or less intimate knowledge of equine nature and homo sapiens' judgment than yours truly has. I've got enough scars and experience to be certain that the homo sap had growed up out of his cave some enlightened. I believe he packed the pony first.

All this must have happened long ago. Let's move up a ways and start looking at the horse-tracks and other sign left by that shadowy figure of history, Genghis Khan. You can go further back in the shadows, but seven

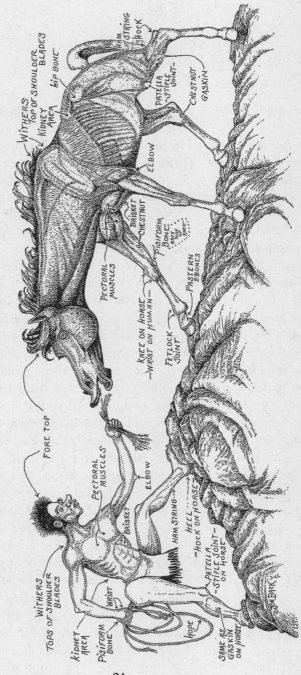

... MAN WITH DESIGNS ON HORSE ...
... WHAT HAVE WE GOT THAT HE HASN'T GOT? ...

Comparative anatomy.

24

hundred years more or less is plenty. Attila the Hun was a warrior horse-man but not in the stature of G. Khan, even if he did come first. This slant-eyed slicker, Mr. Khan, durn near conquered the earth. Now that is taking in a lot of territory, so let's say that he and his helpers worked over a big share of it. This bow-legged bundle of Oriental ambition had more energy and savage lust for power than any other man of his time. He and his men rode over much of the so-called civilized earth.

The horses of Genghis would hardly take prizes at the horse shows of today. Yet you would wonder if ours could compete for stamina with Genghis K's kind of animal.

From what I can glean of the khan's activity and his mobile problems, his herds included, besides horses: yaks, maybe burros, and perhaps camels in the latter part of his exploits. His freighters had carts and other equip-ments, too. So they had mare's milk, horse meat, beef, cow's milk, besides what they could grab along their long route, and boy it must have been long! It has been written that on fast and forced raids, some of these grasp-ing nomads carried small bunches of hay on their saddles (along with other needfuls), and the horse munched his grub on the move. The Mongol warmed his jerked meat between horse and saddle and lunched when he pleased. No coffee time, but, buddy, I'll bet the tea, if they had it, got hell at the stops. I'll bet not many pot-bellied men rode with this outfit—no ulcer pills either or drug stores to get them.

This here tough Mongolian must have had a lot of transportation prob-lems, and he and his hellish helpers had no oiled roads all mapped and ready to travel on. Those boys must have blazed a lot of trails where the eagles lost their way. No, I wasn't there, buddy, but I can tell you where to get the dope on this itchy-footed vandal on horseback. Some histories and faded archives of those times state that a lot of his supplies were hauled in carts, and some mention that much of his cargo was carried on horses, with very little information on the how of it. So I suppose the historians of those days were not packers nor wanted to be. Sharpening their quills was of more importance to them than tieing knots on some snorting old Siberian pony homesick for his grassy Mongolian ranges.

Genghis Khan and his tough hands traveled plenty fast, according to the long-haired men who claim to know. They were about the hardiest and most callous gang in history, and, man, those ponies must have been good. On foot this bunch of bowlegs would have been plumb helpless. The weap-ons these gangsters on horseback used were bow and arrows, spears, and

Trails where the eagles lost their way.

swords—the same weapons the Indians had when the Spanish came ashore. in Mexico three hundred years later. I reckon these fellows were not hampered by rules, either, whether by Hoyle, Queensbury, or Emily Post.

The hit-and-run tactics, the speed with which these Mongols traveled, the use of extra, led-horses for relay use, the transportation of captives and loot, all point to great skill, dexterity, and know-how of the horse. These history-makers must have reinforced their biscuits with horsehair and could pack up while asleep. Didn't take long to stay all night with this layout. And besides their horse skill, you can imagine what these early cavalrymen had to do in the way of keeping up their saddle repairs, their tents, and all the other gear they had to use. They must have had a high skill in tanning hides, weaving wool, and working metal.

The people of those tribes didn't have any more ferocity than the Spaniards who first came to Mexico. But the Spaniard of 300 years after Genghis Khan had guns along with the horse. The Indians didn't yet know of gunpowder and had no knowledge of the horse. If they'd had both those things, the Spaniard might have been suddenly homesick, and Americans might still be living in skin houses and have plenty buffalo.

This comes a little closer to home. The Spaniard who came on the heels of Columbus to conquer and pillage, brought the first horses, mules and burros, and domestic cattle to the New Word. They of course had to transport cargoes of different sorts of supplies as well as the hell raisers themselves—savage warriors who were to show the Indians an undreamed-of fierceness and cruelty coupled with a fearless rapacity for wealth and power.

The hellions themselves had, not long before, thrown off the yoke the Moors had imposed on their native Spain. The Moors, a barbaric people, had brought their own brand of horses and warlike habits to Spain. A lot of these customs were absorbed by the victorious and none too gentle glory-hunting Spaniard. In the 300 years since G. Khan's time, gunpowder with all its accessories had been invented. To the poor Indian, with his weapons not so good as Genghis Khan's, the combination of horse and gunpowder was like the atomic bomb to Hiroshima.

From the time of Hernan Cortes' stepping off the boat in what is now Mexico in the year 1519, along with about sixteen horses and 600 men, things started to pop and sizzle. Mr. Cortes and pardners may not have attended the same sort of Sunday School we did, or else they'd forgotten a lot that they'd learned, of ethics and other qualities most men seem to

27

Bridger and Cortez move on.

admire. But this bird and his followers didn't lack a fanatical courage. They conquered Mexico and overran a good share of the New World.

It was three hundred years after Genghis Khan overran most of Eurasia that Señor Cortes and his men stepped on the shores of Montezuma. Three hundred more years on, Mr. Jim Bridger started taking beaver in the Rockies for the Englishmen's hats in London. He and his like inherited unknowingly and adapted a lot of horse jewelry and customs G. Khan and H. Cortes had used in their conquests.

Let's pause a minute or two to think on the curious mixing of customs and habits when the colonists of mostly English and French nationality met and mingled with the Spanish. Twenty years after Cortes and his horses and men in Mexico, De Soto landed in Florida with horses and men. Less than a hundred years later the English and French started their settlements farther north, bringing over horses and other animals. The Arabian and Barb type of horse of the Spaniards spread north clear to the Oregon country. The slower, heavier horses of the colonists later merged to a certain degree with the Arabian type, as the Americans moved from St. Louis, fur-trading and exploring, to Santa Fe and points west and north. So there is the start of a mixture of not only horse blood, but Spanish and English-French horse equipment, habits of use, and adaptations of all these with the Indians' ideas thrown in.

When the men of the north, Hudson Bay Company trappers working south and west in quest of fur and land, ran out of water for their canoes, and hit land too broken for their Red River carts, they had to turn to the pack horse. The St. Louis issue of fur-trader, trapper, explorer, and hunter also ran out of water for transit and turned to the pack horse. The Santa Fe Spanish type of glory, gold, and fur hunter had never had much water anyway. They had a desert type of country to operate in. They had the jump on the paddle handled raft polers and cart drivers they came in contact with. They had the bulge on the French-Indian-English forest and stream navigators when it came to long experience with the pack horse. Maybe it was easier for the Red River cart drivers and their cousins the boatmen to use Indian travois transportation, but the type of country soon turned them all to the pack horse. The competition was getting more heated. The pace had speeded up. So all three kinds of conquistadores came to rely more on the faster and more mobile transportation.

Maybe you say, what in the name of the Diamond Hitch has all this historical palaver got to do with the pack horse? Well, pardner, if this don't interest you, turn over a few pages and go on from there. When you look at how pack saddles are made, and compare the different kinds—buck, McClelland, army artillery type, and the Decker—this historical stuff has a lot to do with packing the horse. The development of the rigging on a riding or pack saddle, that conglomeration of straps, rings, snaps, buckles, and what your eye detects, is as important as the historical background of that shiny chromium-plated lethal projectile that most of us pay installments on today.

The pack horse himself don't care. He is unaware of and indifferent to all this hullabaloo about his ancestry and his unwanted accessories. He or maybe she don't care a wornout cinch about work or any other type of exertion, any more than the average human. He figures his pastern bones have nothing in common with shock absorbers or knee action. But maybe Henry Ford and his contemporaries and successors have had their inventors turn a furtive eye on his system of propulsion, leverage, and shock absorbancy. Orville Wright and his aerial ancestors and descendants have envied and studied the birds, while the wheeled enthusiasts started with the horse, and the gear he detested and drug around.

More of the methods, equipment, and traditions, and also the names of equipment of both riding and pack saddles seems to me to have come from the Spanish than from any other source. Of course, there are modifications, new ideas, and improved thought on the subject of gear—but basically they most generally point toward Spain.

For instance, in order to get somewhere safely, you may manty up your cargo. That comes from the Spanish *manta,* which means a horse blanket or cover, and refers to wrapping up your oats, meat, or whatever, in a piece of canvas before you put it on the horse. You can see the connection with the lady's *mantilla,* or "little cover."

The pack boxes take their names from several languages. Whether they're made of wood, metal, leather, canvas, plastic, or willow basketry, you'll hear them called "panyards." The word is really "pannier," which is French for bread basket (don't let that horse you're packing kick you in yours!). The Spanish word *alforja* (saddle-bag, pronounced al-for'-hah) is used a lot for the same thing. "Fogeys" they call pack boxes in the southwest—probably came from *alforjas.* The old-time name for pannier, not heard so much these days, is kyack or ki-ack—that's Siwash for pack-sack or pannier.

Aparejo (good Spanish for pack-saddle, pronounced ah-par-ay'-ho) is

30

....GENUINE SQUAW HITCH....

31

still in use. Of course you've got to fasten the *aparejo* to the pack animal, so the *cincha* (girth) and the *latigo* (strap to tighten the cinch) come in handy. We use a lot of Spanish yet in connection with pack outfits.

You can't be so positive about the Diamond Hitch. When you look at all its various forms, uses, and intentions; and also at all the ways to sling, fasten, or hitch loads of cargo to the saddle or the animal's back, you are a quiz kid if you can prove where they came from. Could be a mixture of trials and errors and logic of all the races I've mentioned, plus sea-faring people of many others. The bowline for sure makes you think of ships and the sea. Maybe most of the knots, hitches, slings, and ways to secure fastenings that packers use are also used by sailors, riggers, and other hazardous callings. The best of these and most of them are devised to hold secure when fastened; but rigged so that they don't bind or tangle, and can be untied or disengaged without fumbling, at short notice.

The Indian got in on the deal. It's a simple fact that the horse bred and moved faster than the white man explored. The Spanish horse with his fine high spirits and warm blood showed up in the Siwash-Nez-Perce-Blackfoot country before the white man did, before the Indians living there could even have heard of those gold-hungry and murderous conquistadores of Castile.

Here was these wild four-legged animals with new and undreamed-of possibilities. From well-founded accounts we know that these meat-eating red relatives of ours were using dogs as pack animals and to haul travois. The new big animal, after experiments such as the cave man must have gone through, gave these delighted primitives a new lease on life. They could cover more country and have an easier life. Wider horizons loomed.

They finally evolved a pack saddle which in general principle is much like the ones used today. Parts of elk horns and deer horns where they fork, worked over, served as the bucks or frames, with side bars of wood, fastened and lashed down with soaked rawhide, then dried and shrunk to their constructive tastes. Lo the poor Indian had traded his flat feet for bowlegs, and time has proved he got the best of that deal. So the Indian's invention of the pack saddle, together with the Spanish-English-French and other ideas, are what we inherited.

The Indian hadn't yet heard of woman suffrage, but to quell any feminine uprising the women were designated to suffer as the packers of this new machine. Now that the moccasin is on the other foot, and the men have to do the packing, we'll quit this ancestor-worshipping and get back to work.

32

GETTING ALONG WITH A PACK HORSE

The pack horse we inherited is a mixture, too. He has a short back well equipped to carry a load without sagging (the best ones do), helped to be that way by one less vertebra in the load-carrying area, handed down from an Arabian ancestor; and he has heavy build and weight gotten from the more cold-blooded horse of the colonists from England and France. If you can, pick a good short-backed horse, thick in the body, with strong sturdy legs. A long-pasterned horse cripples up faster than one with short pasterns. You'll find a lot of thin, spindly-legged ponies that'll pack OK but they don't stand up well. Too heavy and too big horses slow you down and are not agile. About a 1200 lb. horse is just right for weight, though lots of smaller horses are used and stay right in the ring. The Morgan type is the boy if you can pick and choose, but don't get too choosey or we'll never get to camp.

The times you'll find that a pack horse comes into camp *intact*, despite very loose cinchas and poor rigging: that horse had a well-fitted saddle and pads and also had a prominent backbone, higher withers, and a well-defined area of the back side of the shoulder blades, plus well shaped chest area and barrel. That is one reason a round, cylindrical-shaped animal, who from hips to shoulder points and all points between is plumb circular, is the animal to stake to somebody else for a pack horse. Don't do this to a good friend you want to keep!

The mind of the horse of today, yesterday, or of several thousand yesterdays hasn't changed or improved up to date any more than our own. He doesn't care any more for work than the average human. The horse like the man has found out through sad and sometimes humiliating experience that work is something he can't get out of. But give him credit for lots of ways and means of trying to avoid it.

Most humans like peace and quiet and more so does the horse. Of course, carrying a heavy load isn't exactly peaceable, but if you keep it quiet, you and the horse will have more peace. It's like buying on the installment plan, to keep it quiet, you pay small installments, and the load isn't noisy. The fine print in the contract, as far as the horse goes, is that long trip.

33

Sometimes a small insurrection turns up.

Each time you unload him, he thinks, "That's it!" But next day, here comes that bill again, I mean halter. You grubstake your horse, that's right, but maybe he thinks your share is kind of high.

All colors, creeds, and dispositions are represented in this longshoreman's division of the equine world. Their union leaders aren't organized, but just watch the pack string, there's a stevedore boss in each one. Sometimes a small insurrection turns up in this line of porters, at which time no small damage is done to poorly packed cargo. Usually the rebellious broomtail who causes it is shown the error of his ways, but sometimes a small flicker in that rolling eye says, "I ain't through yet!"

Sure, the horse is just another animal, but if you don't think that this muscular hay muncher's noodle has more than one idea at a time, you'd better read another book. This wall-eyed pet of ours has a head, four legs, and a tail; in time he can juggle these items in more ways than the tax collector can jiggle your budget.

The big thing the pony thinks of is a full belly, and down to earth that's our main worry, too. You can't shoot a gun with no ammunition. To keep him on the job just watch his back and his belly. Don't overload him and underfeed him and you'll both get home good friends. Leaving him stand with a pack on, or tied up after he's unpacked and hungry "ain't cricket." If the packer expects a long season of packing he has to keep his animals in top shape. So he sees to it that they have time to eat and rest. A jeep eats on the run, and rests in the junk yard if you push it too hard. A horse gets to eat in his spare time, if any, and if you push him beyond reason you walk home, and that poor devil ends up in a coyote or a can.

Most people frown on the idea of eating dog, but to feed a horse to a dog seems to be done in the best circles. Who would connect the echoes of shod hoofs on a rocky canyon trail with the voracious gulps of a flea hunter in the neon lit cliffs of the city? The hunter, at home, gazes with pride at those fine trophies on his walls. He leafs through his album and sees the pack string plowing along through the snowy timbered hills. His trophies and equipment are safely bound on his friend, the trusted pack horse. While he dreams of the fine times and good hunts in those rugged western hills, his wife is in the chain store buying cans of dog food, the remains of his once valued friends, the pack horse and the saddle horse. Life has to go on.

Yessir, when a truck isn't on the road, and it's parked behind the corral, it just sits there. Its work is done until you need it again. When you need

35

it, you jump in and start it up and maybe it goes! Doesn't need to eat except while it works. Everybody knows that. But while that old pony has a few things in common with that beat up old truck, he has to keep right on eating. A few people seem to treat the horse like a truck. They figure to just turn 'em out on rocks and forget 'em. *Then* when they need some work done, just run 'em in and saddle up! Yippee! Strong men and weak horses!

There is many ways to hang, sling, tie, or fasten a pack on one of these lively transports, and we'll get around to them in due time. The way the load is attached to the saddle depends on the kind of burden the cayuse has drawn as his ticket. Usually big heavy horses carry the heaviest loads. Extra gentle and experienced horses are appointed the custodians of the more precious, fragile, and breakable goods. The small horses, and horses with poor backs, and the uncertain boys, get packs not easy to hurt or break, should their imagination overcome their good sense. Not every one of these hairy gents has "horse sense." In fact, quite a few sober and industrious-looking ponies have odd superstitions and peculiar ideas they must eat with the grass. But most of these old boys seem to know that the packer is trying to give them a square deal. After they have had a lot of trails under their shoes, they try to make the best of their lot.

That old saying, "work a good horse to death" applies to a pack horse, but he isn't thinking much about that. He can take a heavy load and be careful of it. A few trips give some horses plenty savvy. Heavy loaded panniers hitting trees or rocks in narrow trails, or sharp turns up and down switchbacks, cause sore hips, shoulders, or bunged-up ribs. A long memory doesn't only occur in an elephant. You'd be surprised at the cat-footed way some of these boys can handle themselves and their packs.

In handling any animal, horse, mule, or burro (I am going to let the experts work with the camels and yaks), you have got to get along with each one's way of thinking—if you want to call it that, and I do. Some people (intellectual monstrosities, maybe) argue that animals besides man don't think or reason. Well, now, my own mentality isn't that far above a horse's, so I am going to be plumb obstinate and say I know different. Enslaved animals, including man, have been known to voice orally or physically their own opinions, even at point of death. Freedom of speech of these pack animals is respected by a good animal man, even though he may not agree and can't bray or whinny.

The bow-legged slavemaster who figures on success without broken bones knows all this, and he allows for the pride, and the public and private whims of these oppressed. To keep all the votes of his four-legged constituents, this two-legged dictator has to be a durned good politician. He knows that some are honest, some crooked, some gentle, some vicious, and some with a grand conglomeration of all these qualities. There is also a lot of politicians among horses and mules. What we sometimes mistake for affection is a four-legged politician doing his stuff. They have real affection for their own kind, but what they exhibit toward the human is pure wile. If you are a stern disciplinarian and also a benevolent despot, you'll make the grade. Give them hard work, good treatment, and plenty of respect, and they'll respond in kind. Give them hard work and a dirty deal—you'll get paid in full, sometimes sudden.

I've seen people who pack up their string, take for the hills, trot their packed ponies along, up and down steep tough country, never give 'em a breather on steep grades, pound them thirsty across the creeks, never straighten a slipped pack or tighten a loose cinch—and if and when they reach their camp site, keep them tied to trees till dark, some of them still with their packs on. These birds lots of times wrangle their stock early in the a.m., rush them into the corral, and tie them to the trees again. Then, after 3 or 4 hours, these sadists start slapping their oversize packs and undersize pads on their beloved helpers. Never shake out the twigs and pine needles or scrape off the hair and dried sweat out of the blankets and pads. Nor do they see the kidney sores or cinch cuts they've made or started. They turn 'em loose with a lot of whoopin' and hollerin' and whip them up the trail. Boy! It's a great life that these gents with the undersized brains in the oversize hats live in the great outdoors. Whoopee! Let 'er buck!

Thank the good Lord that there are few of these. Maybe when they are run in by the final Wrangler, they are tied to trees, a little high and permanent.

There are all kinds of horses, and the good packer gets along with them all. You'll encounter sway backs, rat backs, straight backs, barrel shapes (some rounder than a barrel if that can be), straight bellies, pot bellies, shad bellies, and some of a shape that even Hollywood wouldn't believe. Most all can be fitted with a saddle, and if you use good judgment as to adjustment of equipment, will transport your cargo.

This is not a dissertation on the kind, build, habits, construction, and mental and spiritual qualities of pack animals, but on getting them to do what you need to have them do, so let's get into that.

Apprentice on way to kindergarten.

The first, cheapest, and most valuable lesson a pack horse can learn is to be broke to picket. The best part of the deal is that the horse does all the work. He is self educated. There is a lot of ways people have of halter breaking the horse, but that doesn't picket break him. Some birds rig up rope contraptions, pulley deals, gadgets, and harness outfits to teach a horse to lead. They do most of the labor themselves. Picket breaking also halter breaks this snorty machine. It's been in use a long time, whoever worked it out is long gone and unknown.

Catch the green pony, put a strong halter with a big halter ring on it, on his brain box. Get a good strong soft rope, one inch or bigger in diameter. Run one end through the halter ring and tie a fairly snug bowline around his neck. Now heave, haul, drag, and anyhow get him tied to the middle of a 12-inch log, 20 feet or more long. Have the log trimmed, with no knots sticking out, and have it out in advance in the middle of a park, meadow, or smooth piece of ground, where he can't get tangled up with anything but himself and maybe the log.

Only one out of a hundred jerks a neck down or ever hurts anything but his pride. He'll run, bust himself, tangle himself, get up, think, try it again and again. After more acrobatic flip-flops, kicks, and bucks than Ringling

Introduction to teacher.

Tangled up with teacher.

Graduated.

and Tom Mix ever dreamed of, he gives up. A couple of days of this, and he has more education and value than you could manually give him in a week.

Some gents rope a large, strong spring to the log, and tie the picket rope to the spring. When the pony hits the end of the rope, the spring takes up some of the jar.

Anyhow, all these didoes and houlihans this first grader goes through with teach him to lead, and I don't mean maybe. They also teach him that getting wound up, fouled up, tangled up, and hobbled with his big rope don't hurt him. (Be sure to use a big soft rope so he won't burn himself.) They give him an expert knowledge of picketing. This is the best preliminary training for a rope horse there is. You can drag wood on him. If you are a packer, you need wood in camp, and how.

Myself, I'd rather picket by a front foot with a picket broke horse, than by the neck. Less trouble if you do it right. *But*, you must break him to the picket log *first*, by the *neck*.

Don't turn any of your stock loose with a halter on, if they are shod. An animal can get into a jackpot which can ruin him. Many times a shod horse, loose or on a picket, scratches his ear or head with a hind foot,

40

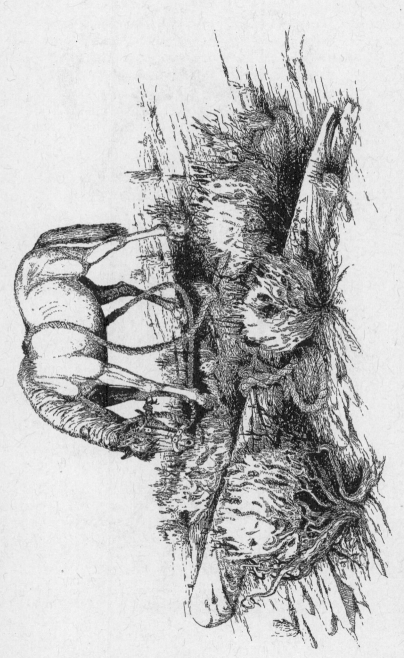

Teacher's pet.

41

...To Picket a Shod Horse By The Halter,

...Is Risky...

..It's Safer To Picket By The Foot..

42

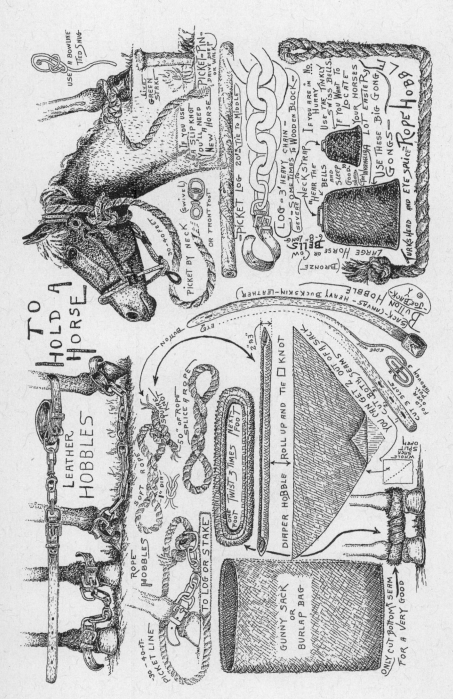

43

...TIEING UP A HIND LEG...

...TIEING UP A HIND LEG...

44

catches some part of the halter with a heel cork or shoe end. Then he gets the halter wedged between the hoof and shoe and down he goes. If it doesn't slip loose quick and you don't find him sooner, he'll claw with the hung foot and cork, and cut himself with the loose hind foot till he is bunged up bad, or worse.

When I reach camp, I like to picket a couple of horses on good feed, by the foot, then bell the rest and turn them loose.

Many people like to use hobbles, and some use side lines. Hobbled horses get used to the hobbles, and some can take the lead in a bunch of fast moving horses, and travel for miles. Hobbles, used too much and too long, can cause stiff and sored up pasterns, and make heel cuts. Side lines, which are used on left front and left hind feet, or right front and right hind, slow up a horse's travel. A side-lined horse can seldom travel as far as a hobbled horse. There are many more styles of hobbles than I have illustrated. Many good, comfortable, and lasting hobbles can be made out of odds and ends of material at hand. The principle of hobbles and handcuffs is the same. Hobbles of gunny sacks or burlap bags are about the cheapest to make. Keep your leather hobbles oiled with neat's foot oil. Any hobbles, especially gunny sack and rope, are onery to handle when wet or shrunken or half-frozen.

We'll assume that most of the horses we are using here are well broke: but we'll probably find a few that resent having a pack slapped on their carcasses. There are several ways of convincing one of these gold bricks that you can change his viewpoint without hurting him or you.

One of the best ways to do it is to tie up a hind leg. Take about twenty feet or more of 5/8 inch or large soft rope, and throw one end around his neck, above the shoulders. Tie a bowline low on the left side, forming a loose collar. Slip the other end through this collar, and with the resulting loop, snare his right hind foot. The left will do, but the right works better. Work from the left side. Now snare a hind foot just below the fetlock, and pull up his hind leg a foot or more off the ground. Tie a slip double half hitch to hold him. If he gets tough, hist his leg higher. Now saddle and pack him. If he hops around too much, tie your jacket on his forehead, just over his eyes. Pull the sleeves through the halter cheek pieces and fold under snug. This is fairly fast, and easy on him and you. Get him packed, then tail him up to a calm strong horse, and take blindfold and leg rope off. He has graduated into teacher's pet.

Sometimes this blindfold deal and tieing up a hind leg has to be done

45

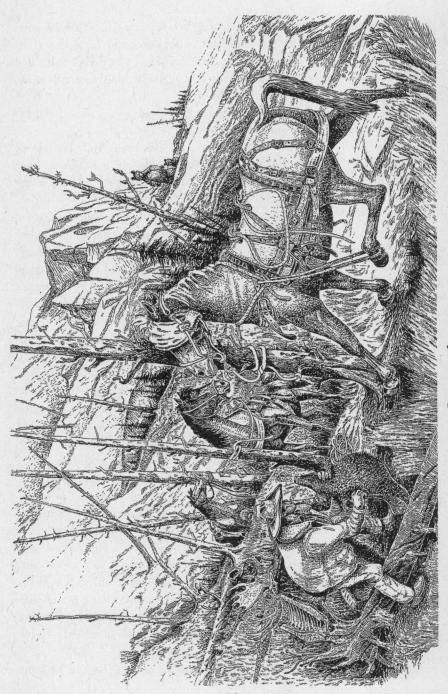

Leg up and no see.

46

··THE RUNNING W··

··IN USE··

often, when packing fresh-killed game, especially bear. Dead bear, grizzly in particular, seem to spook most horses, as much as live ones do. Lots of packers smear blood on the nose of a snuffy horse as a sort of local anesthetic. Then that's all he smells, *you hope*. This works on any kind of meat to be packed, *sometimes*. Often it quiets down his superstitions.

Now here is the way to pack the toughest pony there is. This rarely has to be done, and, Bud, don't try it on *fragile cargo*. It works OK with frozen meat, or with cargo that can't be hurt. Start by tieing up a hind leg and blindfolding him, then tie his front legs together, saddle him, and *cinch tight*. Now slip your halter rope through this hobble, pull his head down, and tie the rope with a slip-hitch. Then pull him down and on his side. Sling your one side pack. Tie it on snug, and through a swing ring on a cinch. Now roll him clear on over, and he is resting on your one side pack. Now sling and tie the remaining side pack. Done on soft footing and careful, it isn't hard on anything except his pride. Let him up, and he has got his diploma.

The *Running-W* is as old as the hills, but some people may not have come in contact with it. In breaking a horse it comes in handy, especially for a wagon or work horse. But it also has its value in working with a green saddle horse or pack-horse-to-be. You can see in my drawing what it will do. You can hang a cinch ring in the middle of the front cinch, and use the swing side rings on the cinch of a saddled horse if you want to.

But for teaching a bronc or spooky pony to let you pack him, tieing up a hind leg is hard to beat.

Another way to control a horse is to rig a strait jacket. You have to use strong breeching and breast collars. On the left side, connect the breast collar with an adjustable heavy strap to the breeching ring. On the right side, rig a 3/8 inch strong rope and small pulley from the breast collar to the breeching ring for a draw rope. Adjust the left strap snug. You can draw his shoulder and hip sections inactive. Adjust the breast collar and breeching low down.

A note on handling mules: if you are able to own or use mostly mules, it is necessary to keep a good smart bell mare as hostess, lure, mother confessor, and Emily Post. It means easier wrangling and steadier disposition. Hunting for strays and lost ones is almost nil, as long as you can keep the bell mare from straying. She won't stray if she's a good picket horse. In the frosty morning the long-eared gang brays, "We're all here, pardner!"

There's lots of gentle mules, but they've got a sardonic sense of humor,

···STRAIT JACKET···
···LEFT···

···STRAIT JACKET···
···RIGHT···

There's lots of gentle mules.

if you can call it that. It pays to rule them with a firm hand, maybe even a firm grip on a club sometimes. I know of a packer hired to work mules. When the boss asked him why he hadn't got one mule's tail out from under the britchen, the packer said the mule kicked him when he tried. The boss picked up a heavy lash rope, doubled it, and whanged the mule four or five times across his rump, then calmly pulled the mule's tail from under the britchen. The boss looked at the packer and said, "Before you work with some mules you gotta get their attention! Their long ears make 'em absent-minded."

When you have to work on one, work on his rump, not his head. When your gas buggy stalls, you don't take a hammer to the distributor, do you? Maybe I'm prejudiced, but it seems to me there are more chancy and sneaky characters among mules than among horses. If you are scared of them, keep it under your hat.

THIS IS THE GEAR

Some people believe that a pack horse has no more problems than a plow horse, or a work horse on a wagon. While there is some relation, the job to be done just isn't the same. The load is on his back, he isn't pushing or pulling it. Lots of times he can be led, but there is a good many circumstances where he can only be turned loose to follow or be driven. A work horse is driven by lines, or hooked to others that are, and is mostly guided by hand to do the job. A pack horse has to use his mind mostly, along with his weighted back and feet. He has problems to work out that the work horse leaves to the driver.

He has a harness, more complicated than the saddle horse's. Some humans doing cruel hard work wear suspenders and no belt, some wear both. Most people wear clothes, so they have to hold them on somehow. A horse, mule, or burro, who is carrying a load, has to wear a breast collar, a britchen, and two belts, sometimes three. That word britchen, or breeching, sounds like breeches, and he does wear it in the same area of his anatomy; but he wouldn't be caught dead with a pair of pants on.

You can see that as the loaded pack horse travels along he has a load on his back and on his mind, too. When he goes downhill, his saddle and load move forward; so you have that breeching around his hips adjusted to keep the load from going too far forward. When he goes uphill, the breast collar should be adjusted to counteract the slipping back. As this four-legged freighter moves forward, his cinches loosen as he burns up some soft fat off his ribs. Naturally this work makes him thirsty. He drinks at every creek even if he isn't thirsty. This tightens the cinchas a little. A good packer should watch them close.

Some packers don't use either britchen or breast collars. Once on a trip to British Columbia and Alberta I noticed some packers in very rough country who seemed to be doing OK without either on their pack saddles. The front cinches were plumb tight, and the back cinch was tight and far back on the belly. I didn't see much top pack on their animals. Pot-bellied

THIS IS THE GEAR

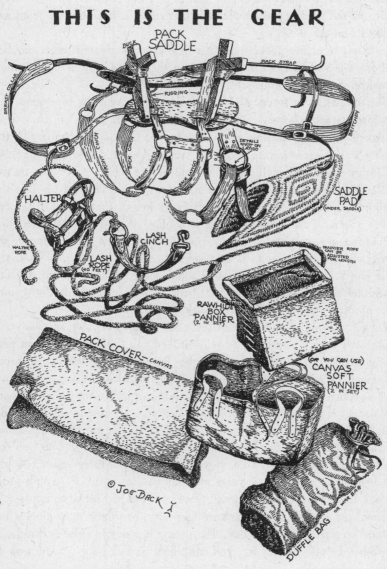

PACK SADDLE

BUCK

PACK STRAP

RIGGING

BREAST COLLAR

FRONT CINCH

BACK CINCH

FRONT LATIGO

BACK LATIGO

DETAILS KNOT ON LATIGO

BRITCHEN

HALTER

HALTER ROPE

LASH CINCH

LASH ROPE (40 FEET)

SADDLE PAD (UNDER SADDLE)

PANNIER ROPE CAN BE ADJUSTED FOR LENGTH

RAWHIDE BOX PANNIER (2 IN SET)

PACK COVER — CANVAS

(OR YOU CAN USE) CANVAS SOFT PANNIER (2 IN SET)

© JOE BACK

DUFFLE BAG OR WAR BAG

horses seemed to be favored. The idea is that the pot belly and the architecture of the rib cage eliminates the need of breast collars in front and holdbacks on the stern.

Some other places packers use a single cinch and a britchen on their saddles. The saddle sits a little ahead on the animal and is rigged about centerfire. Some Canadians do it this way.

Most of the no-britchen, no-breast-collar boys favor no top packs, and therefore use more horses. Do it your own way, but bring 'em back alive.

Picture your pony fording a stream—maybe he has to swim it. All this rushing water forces him to scramble over and around big slimy boulders and soggy muck. After this delightful adventure he has to jump over fallen timber, tangled roots, and steep slide rock. You can just bet that this continuous revelry is no picnic. Everybody knows that a dance like this doesn't go on all the time, but there is enough of it to show the need our harried friend has to have a good rig, well-adjusted, his load balanced, and placed where it should be. It also suggests the real usefulness of breast collar and britchen. This acrobat of the timbered hills needs an A-1 diamond hitch all around his load; but if the pack is not balanced and slung right, no diamond hitch is worth a packer's damn!

When you rare back and gaze at those corded muscles, that big body and those sturdy legs, if you haven't been initiated you think the pony can pack enormous loads. But the fact is that the homo sap on just two legs can pack much more in proportion to his weight than his four-legged partner can do. When you pack 80 or 90 pounds of cargo on each side of a pack animal, that is plenty. Sometimes 200 pounds on a horse is OK, but it depends on the kind, size, weight, and condition of the animal. Remember, you also have a pad or two, a pack saddle with rigging, and a halter on this long-suffering bird. Now, Bud, if you don't believe these estimates, just pack in rough country a few years and find out for yourself. You'll probably say 150 pounds on a broomtail is all he should be asked to haul.

Sometimes a small animal, mature and wiry, can pack more than a big one, and keep it up day after day. But pack a horse light if he is still growing. When he gets his growth, you can't hurt him so easy. No minors allowed.

The footwork a pack horse has to do isn't in a boxer's class, and he does have the advantage of four feet; but some of the places he is asked to go, with that *dead weight* strapped to his back, would scare a combination of Jack Dempsey and Strangler Lewis out of the fight. The saddle horse has a *live weight* on his back; if he has a good hand aboard to ease him over the trouble spots, he has more chance than a harassed pack animal.

Many people at some time in their lives have come in contact with a tailor who makes clothes for them. With that tape slung along his withers, this gent sizes up the two-legged egotist who is going once for all to have his manly carcass decorated and really appreciated as he knows dern well it hasn't been in the past. This canny tailor gent wasn't born yesterday. Mebbe unknown to himself he has more knowledge of anatomy than that sawbones who took our your gizzard when you were ailing. Mebbe you have a sway back and pot belly, though you wouldn't admit it even to yourself. Now this bird, like the packer, sizes you up in a hurry, but he don't let on, like the packer does. When he gets done, your pack is on where it should be, your cinchas do their work, your leadups and holdbacks fit to a horsehair. When you trot along your trails, even the Moose and Elk lodge members look up—and feel that their food tastes better than ever before!

While I have never seen or heard of a tailor turned packer, I feel that if one did he'd be a good hand at this game.

A lot of people don't put their pads or blankets far enough forward, under the saddle or pack saddle. The bars on the riding or pack saddle fit just behind the animal's shoulder blades, where there is movement of muscles and hide, plus the jar of the gait. So place your blankets and pads 3 or more inches in front of the forward edge of the saddle bars. If cinchas get too loose, pads (especially new ones), slip back; and boy, you are in as much trouble as the poor horse. Think of the tailor.

So, when you finally adjust, cuss, tighten up, loosen up, and really fix your hairy customer's pads, saddle, breast collar, britchen, and cinchas, and *know* they're right—then print Ole Roany's name on this uniform!

Sway-backed and high-withered horses require more padding to be comfortable than hog-backed horses do. Some barrel-shaped horses are very hard to pack at all; you better sling the pack very low and use no top packs. Some of them fit up like a saddle on a sow.

The cinch area of a pack animal varies a lot; across the sternum or breastbone from about the 6th to 12th rib of the horse is about right. If you pack mares or pot-bellied horses the cinchas aren't hard to keep in place. On a shad- or thin-bellied horse, some packers connect the center of double cinchas with a 6- or 8-inch latigo strap or string to keep the back cinch from slipping too far back.

Many times, after a packer has run his horses or mules in, and has slapped his packsaddles on them and fed them a little oats, it's a while till they are loaded. So always make it a habit of casting your weather eye over each rig to be sure it's OK, then cinch up tight, plenty tight, *just before* you start to put your packs on the animal. If you forget to cinch up tight, you can figure out for yourself the rest of it. I have seen birds, just after they saddle up the outfit, cinch the horses or mules up plenty tight, then fiddle around *for three or four hours before* they put on the cargoes. That is plumb dumb! Hard on the critters for nothing. If you cinch up plenty tight *just before* you load a pony, and then take off, the movement of horse and load, plus some shrinkage of horse and load and a little stretch, will ease the horse while in motion. Use good wide cinchas. When a cinch wears out, have some extras at hand or make repairs. A fishcord cinch, worn half in two, tightened around a horse's belly, is a sadist's delight.

It doesn't take a brain truster out of the Pentagon to get used to properly fitting a pack saddle and padding and gear to most any horse or his long-eared cousin. So let's talk about the pack saddles themselves.

PACK SADDLES

You have a choice of pack saddles, so along this part of the trail we should ponder on the kinds you may use. There are several kinds, and to different packers each kind may be good, bad, or indifferent. After trying them out, you'll form your own preference; and although sometimes the pack pony may not agree, he won't say so in words. The sawbuck, the Decker with its canvas pouch pads, the McClellan, various army artillery surplus saddles, plus some homemade pack saddles—these are what you usually have a choice of. You can pack a lot of different cargo on a riding saddle, too. We'll go into that a little later.

The sawbuck saddle is most like the one the Indians devised; it has wooden cross-pieces front and back (where the Indians used the forks of deer or elk horns), and carved wooden side bars. Just because one of these resembles in construction that old woodcutter's pride, the sawbuck,, doesn't mean it has both uses. I believe that of all the kinds and types of pack saddles used in this country and Canada you'll find more of that good old standby, the sawbuck, used than any other. There are many advantages, and, some say, improvements in some of the others. But that old sawbuck, well-constructed, with good well-shaped side bars, with a wool-skin lining, and wide enough in buck construction for average animals, is just hard to beat for general packing. When it's rigged even and accurate, of A-1 leather, with snaps, rings, and buckles that can be adjusted to suit the build of the particular animal, with comfortable cinchas, and breast collar and britchen OK, you can move a lot of cargo.

The front and rear tips of the bars of some pack saddles don't turn up enough to avoid digging into the shoulder blades or withers of the animal—too straight along the inner side of the bar. They should be able to rock just a little, especially in front. You can pare them off a little, and curl them at the front a trifle. Homemade packsaddles are few and far between, and most have poorly designed bars. The Decker packsaddle bars can be adjusted somewhat at the hoops—a reason why many packers like the Decker.

The McClellan type army saddles of the first world war were cheap, and

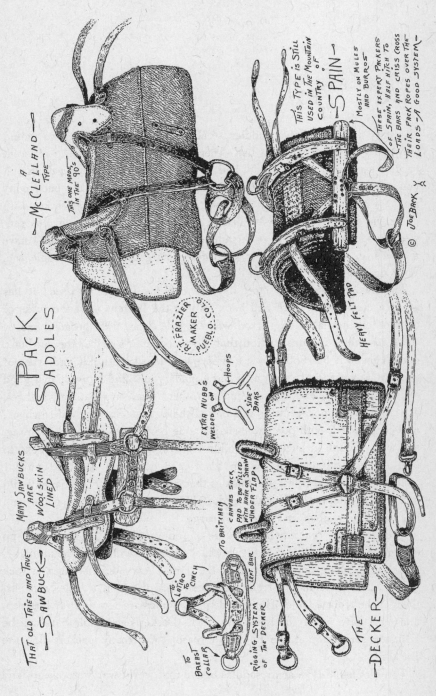

PACK SADDLES

— McCLELLAND TYPE —

A McCLELLAND TYPE —

THIS ONE MADE IN THE 90'S

R. FRAZIER MAKER PUEBLO. CO.

THIS TYPE IS STILL USED IN THE MOUNTAIN COUNTRY OF

— SPAIN —

MOSTLY ON MULES AND BURROS

THESE EXPERT PACKERS OF SPAIN, HALF HITCH TO THE BARS AND CRISS CROSS THEIR PACK ROPES OVER THE LOADS — A GOOD SYSTEM —

© JOE BACK

HEAVY FELT PAD

THAT OLD TRIED AND TRUE — SAWBUCK —

MANY SAWBUCKS ARE WOOLSKIN LINED

EXTRA NUBB'S WELDED ON

— HOOPS

SIDE BARS

TO BRITCHEN

CANVAS SACK

PAD TO BE FILLED WITH HAIR OR STRAW UNDER FLAP —

TO LATIGO TO CINCH

LEAT BAR

TO BREAST COLLAR

RIGGING SYSTEM OF THE DECKER

THE — DECKER —

well made for adaptation as pack saddles. Lots of them can still be found. Most people strip off the rigging and straps these good trees come equipped with and re-rig and re-equip them to use as pack saddles. I have done this, and have had a lot of use and luck with them. The quality of so-called army russet leather is to my mind very poor and weak. Throw this away and get good latigo leather and a few buckles and rings, and rig you up some serviceable and comfortable saddles.

Some of the last war's web belting, canvas, and metal boxes fit in very well to make a good serviceable outfit. These can be used for years, and are very reasonable in price and sound in quality. If you want to see a pleased little boy, just examine a squint-eyed hillbilly ramming and fumbling around a well-stocked war surplus store. This gent peers, mumbles, jerks, fondles the heavy canvas sacks, all sizes; straps, all lengths and widths; stoves, tents, steel and wooden boxes, artillery saddles, pots and pans, kitchen artillery, mysterious looking gadgets, and conglomerations of everything. The storekeeper may be suspicious and puzzled; but this is just a normal packer who is for a while in Paradise. Boy, there is a lot of articles handy and cheap for the price that can be adapted for horse jewelry and fundamental needs.

EQUIPMENT

When a bunch of nature lovers or hungry hunters, bent on traveling through these timbered hills and snow-capped peaks, show up at some bow-legged gent's ranch, and say, "Let's go!"—this squint-eyed yap's trouble starts. Oh, sure, he's an optimist, or he'd choose an easier life.

These birds with the $100 fish poles and their trusty rifles need a lot of gear to keep them happy. Radios and cameras, boxes of bottles, toilet gear, clothes, reading matter, fishing gear, bed rolls, and a lot of other odds and ends—and then food, tents, lanterns, gasoline, tools, folding chairs and tables, mattresses, stoves, and 101 other things. Oh, that poor old pack string.

The packer who stays in business always tries to take the long view of it, where the impulsive and the know-it-alls may jump in without looking ahead. The packer has to figure on length of trip, kind of country, trail condition, time or miles between camps, the horse feed known or thought to be available; amount of food, gear, tents or shelter to be taken. The number of horses available and the amount and kind of cargo to be packed is the big item. On a fast trip in tough country the food, shelter, personal needfuls, and all other gear, are condensed into only the essentials.

We've all heard people, fed up with whatever they have bothering them, say, "I'm going to take off for a while, and *get away from it all!*" Yes, sir, we've probably all said that, but when we go to "get away from it all" we furtively load up some special things that we've just gotta have. We don't want to get away from *everything*. Well, there's a saying that whether you're in Rome, Georgia, or Rome, Italy, "when in Rome do as the Romans do," and if you're a packer you may have to say, "This is Rome, Wyoming." On a trip anywhere there are things you need and things you can get along without. If you've got plenty of room, and weight is no problem, you can take the extras. But with a bunch of horses there is only so much room. Weight and bulk are both problems. So take what you really need; then if there is any room left, you can get away from it all with a few more items you just gotta have. All this depends on the number and kind of horses available. Enough horses with light packs makes for a better trip than not enough horses with heavy and top packs.

Well, let's get going. Let's figure how many mouths to feed, for how long, and let's hope nobody's on a diet. Maybe those flyrods can be used to catch trout with—that'll help. Of course, you can't eat hunting and fishing licenses, but they don't weigh much and are handy to have around.

The men who make a business of guiding, outfitting, and packing hunters, fishermen, surveyors, and others out into the tall timber and high peaks usually have a list. (See Appendix.) It'll be a time-tried list of how much and what kind of food and supplies are needed for a known number of people and a specified time. Some outfits figure that for a fairly long trip, say ten days or more, it takes about a horse and a half per person, to pack food, shelter, bedding, and personal effects. So, if my 8th grade figures are still OK, it takes fifteen pack horses for ten people. Each, of course, has to have a saddle horse besides, or twenty-five riding and pack horses for ten people; and for that long a trip we'd better take a couple of spares.

For hunting trips enough oats should be taken along for a couple of good feeds a day for each animal. Takes more food for man or beast than those leisurely summer trips in warmer and better weather. You've got tougher weather, harder work, longer days, and less time for the animals to collect that grass which they earn many times over. It pays to take some grain even on summer trips, for small feeds for the hard-working wrangle horse, extra feed on fast trips and on poor grass, and for a come-on to keep them from straying.

Some outfits neglect to take stock salt along with them. Horses have to have it, and it helps to hold them close to the camp. Lots of times the salt ground is a good place for unusual pictures of game animals, lured in by that irresistible attraction.

Just about now is the time to mention this—don't forget to bring axe and shovel and a log saw. If you forget to bring a good 10-inch or 12-inch file you'll be sorry. Bring hammer, spikes for corral poles, haywire for stovepipe rigging, and a pair of pliers.

BALANCING THE LOAD

You've heard me mention balance before—more than once. If you don't balance each load, it's your hard luck. The handiest and cheapest tool you can buy is a fairly accurate spring or other scale that will take weights up to 100 or 150 pounds. It will last for years and you'll always use it. Some people like the style with a hook at the bottom and a ring or handle at the top. Seven or eight bucks for one will save you and your outfit a million dollars worth of grief.

Balance the two sides of each pack, being sure they weigh the same, whether they're panniers, side packs of any kind, mantied cargo, bedrolls, tents, or any daggoned ordinary pack you load. And say, Bud, you'll be surprised how much of a liar the scales make you out to be, no matter how good a guesser you think you are. Then hang or sling these balanced loads on the saddle at the same height.

If you are a darn good guesser or have used a scale you are ready to start packing. The long and short of it is, that no matter how good you are at tieing the final hitch, if your packs are not well balanced and even, your pretty diamond won't insure you a steady engagement.

A pack animal has to be packed as comfortable as possible, and still carry a pay load. His burden should be carried on the top of the sides of his rib cage, not too far back, not too far forward, or you'll hamper his action. Don't let these statements puzzle you, pardner; I am just trying to put a bee in your bonnet, with the stinger removed. I'm not about to be a prim-lipped humane officer, neither am I trying to spook you about this deal. There are real reasons: if you pack your load too high you won't go far before it slips; if you pack your load too low, you will squeeze his torso and hamper his breathing machine, and he ain't agoin' to love you no more. You may end up pitching your camp ten miles short of where you figured on going. Don't trade your bed for a lantern.

We have all noticed how a good jockey on his race horse wears short stirrups and leans forward over his horse's withers. He is giving his horse all the help he can. The horse governs, guides, and handles himself with his front quarters. His hind quarters are the propelling unit. The jockey's

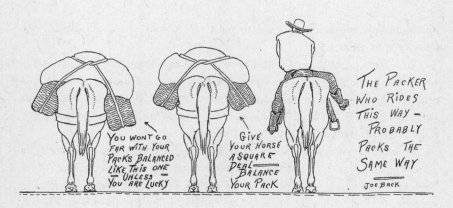

YOU WONT GO FAR WITH YOUR PACKS BALANCED LIKE THIS ONE — UNLESS — YOU ARE LUCKY

GIVE YOUR HORSE A SQUARE DEAL — BALANCE YOUR PACK

THE PACKER WHO RIDES THIS WAY — PROBABLY PACKS THE SAME WAY

JOE BACK

... BALANCE YOUR SADDLE ...

weight is kept away from the horse's kidney area, and his breathing ability is helped as much as possible. This pack pony of yours is no race horse, but he's got the same anatomy. The pack won't help him, but it's got to hinder him as little as possible.

Have you noticed riders who rare back against the cantle no matter what the gait? Up hill, down hill, all their weight always on the kidneys? They sit on one side of the saddle, then the other. Jog, jog, jog! Bang, bang, bang! Just watch these birds. All they ever use the stirrups for is to get on or off. When that big pie or sore place shows up right sudden on that pore old pony's back, they ignore it or figger somebody put porcupine eggs in their blankets. Never give that four-legged sucker a break. The bird who rides back on his cantle and doesn't help his mount over rough spots is the same as a dead weight pack on a horse. If your pack is too high and too far back, as the horse walks along, the pack will sway and weave too much, and put too much wear on his back and kidney area—all same as the poor type of rider.

The rider who habitually rides on one side and then the other, does the same to a horse as a pack load that is heavy on one side and light on the other. When you put an unbalanced load on a pony, he flinches and moves over to brace himself. If it puzzles you, it sure as hell don't puzzle the horse. It's his carcass that hurts, not yours.

Speaking of balancing a load, what do you think your *saddle horse* feels about that big bunch of nothing he's packing up hill and down dale? Maybe you've got a pair of those big army saddle bags right over your horse's kidneys, packed with a lot of odds and ends you don't really need. There's a big heavy coat, buckled and tied behind the cantle. A rifle with a telescope sight is in that scabbard under your left leg. A hunting axe or hatchet is tied on the right side skirts. There is also a neck rope or halter, a bridle, a 40-pound saddle, YOU, complete with clothes, boots, binoculars, ammunition, ulcer pills, hunting knife, and a burning desire for the biggest and best head that will bust the trophy book wide open. *That,* pardner, is a load that takes a big, strong, grained-up horse, if you use him every day.

To my way of operating, the best way to pack your rifle is butt up and back, muzzle down and ahead, in your scabbard under your left leg and stirrup leathers. Pack your rope, hatchet, and whatever else it takes to balance the gun and scabbard, on the right or opposite side. Then, if you favor your horse a little, you can put a lot of ups and down in your memory book, and still get the job done.

PACKING UP RIGHT

Does the human live who hasn't seen some worried looking man or woman hustling along with a bulging suitcase or bag of some sort, from which socks or undies peek out forlornly at the interested spectator? Maybe the hurry was the tax collector, or the sheriff, or the guy was late for the doings at the minister's house and had forgot the ring.

Packing a suitcase or a bag of groceries right has some connection with packing panniers to fit a horse or mule. Quite a few times I've seen potatoes, busted eggs, kitchen hardware, torn up blankets, and other needfuls, scattered along a trail and hanging to tree limbs and snags. Now, pull up your pony when you see this. Mebbe you won't have to; your hungry nag is already nibbling at those oats dribbled among the pebbles on the dusty trail. Listen, you can hear some bird hollering up ahead at some snorting horses crashing through the spruce jungle on the mountain side. Mebbe this has happened to your own string. It has to mine. In a grocery store or hotel, a revolving door or a counter corner could snag your bag of plunder, but the damage wouldn't be so hard to take. You could pack up or replace most of your stuff; but out in the tall and uncut, things are different.

Of course, mebbe it wasn't carelessness or ignorance that caused the uproar. You may just round a corner in the trail and find a yellow-jacket's or bald-headed hornet's nest that a bear has real lately pulled the top off of; good packin' and good gear won't call off the rodeo, but they'll sure shorten the patch-up afterwards. Or mebbe some jittery pony tried to crowd past the one ahead on a narrow tree-lined trail. A pannier corner hits a tree and busts a britchen strap, or both horses have a squeezing catch. The trees don't give, but something packed on the ton or so of grunting horseflesh does, something has gotta give. Sure, mebbe the packs and gear is shipshape and packed right. But lots of times the trouble is poor packs and flimsy gear. Poor packs even with good gear can be poison; it'll surprise you how fast a good gentle horse can buck and kick its way out of an outfit slipped under its belly. The gear can usually be patched up somehow; the damage to the horse is often permanent. Anyhow, Bud, we're a long way from that grocery store, and I just saw that shod buckskin kick the hell out of that dragging bedroll of yours!

You wouldn't expect that some Rocky Mountain pine squirrel would line her nest with eiderdown from Arctic birds, but it has happened. A sober friend of mine swears he saw a Wyoming raven flying through the timber sporting a monocle on one eye—a Zeiss lens at that. Oh, yes, another guy I know, who pushes pack ponies for a living, claims he once saw a young female grizzly humped up on a rocky ledge looking for a lost mate. She had a pair of battered up field glasses to help her poor eyesight. So he says. These items musta come from wrecked packs along the trails.

Let's say you done a good job, and made it to camp all right, only a little later than you counted on. When you've unpacked your kitchen and grub pile, be sure to know what pannier or pack has your hobbles, horse bells, side lines, and extra halters; you'll use a lash rope for a picket rope. There's nothing meaner than rummaging around through a lot of packs and panniers for gear that you need sudden and now! Maybe you didn't bring 'em? Hold up a minute, Bud, brush the snow off that pack, hold your candle a little higher. Yep, there they are!

Well, you done right. You stuffed scrap paper or gunnysack up in and around all the clappers on the horse bells, and included in one pannier the hobbles, rope, bells, horseshoes, and tools, wrapped up in extra pads and canvas; and balanced it against the other pannier with spuds in it. Your tepee made a top pack. The pole axe in its scabbard helped to balance the spuds. Just right. Now you can cut a green stake to picket your wrangle horse in that park close to camp. Drive it down deep! If you take a double-bitted axe, too, you can really do business: one edge for rough work, the other for clean.

Some pack animals don't mind rattles, but most of them do. If you wrap and pad all metal things from each other, and put them in panniers away from contact with the animal, you make better time. The present day horse knows all about the atomic bomb. You know how people talk. Besides, he gets the lowdown from papers the litterbugs scatter around the country. These animals weren't born yesterday. They are right on the ball. Some of them hear two frying pans dance a jig with a couple of loose butcher knives, and figger that if a rattlesnake didn't crawl in that pannier last night, it must be one of them infernal machines a-tickin' away. There's that old saying, "if you stop to think": well, a horse figures why stop to think, might as well do it on the run. So he takes off, branches and limbs

66

a-poppin' and rocks a-clatterin'. By the time you get him caught, *you* are a-rattlin'. Pad the rattles.

Old Squint-eye has through the years developed a good system of packing food or anything else anyone needs in the mountains.

Packing cans is a cinch. And as most people live out of cans nowadays, we'll use 'em, too. Take about five ordinary cans, lay them end to end on a gunny sack laid out flat, fold back the slack at the ends, roll up tight, and tie with two cords hard and fast. Use this system with all your tinned food. (These gunny sacks are used in camp in a lot of ways—hobbles, cinchas, repairs, doormats, so when you've got the food used up, you and the horses have wore out the gunny sacks. Take plenty. If you don't wear them out you can use them again.) Pack these long rolls of cans horizontal in panniers, the heaviest on the bottom. If you don't wrap and insulate your cans this way, you may find all the labels rubbed loose. You may open up peas when you wanted peaches. It pays to wrap, fold, and insulate.

All your food that comes in cardboard boxes (oatmeal, cornmeal, etc.), should be placed in separate cotton sacks and tied tight, or wrapped in newspapers and tied snug. Sugar, salt, flour, raisins, rice, and coffee should be double-sacked and tied tight. Clean flour and salt sacks are wonderful for this. If you like sugar, flour, salt, coffee, raisins, and rice all jumbled up together when you open a pack, you ain't the kind of bird I thought you was! When your pack custodian goes up and down trails, he picks up his feet and puts them down. For jar on dead weight, he durn near equals a postal clerk.

A good way to pack eggs is to take them out of the cartons, wrap and twist each one in a couple of squares of toilet paper, fairly loose, and put them back in the cartons. Most cartons come with the bottom half fitted to the eggs. If you'll cut the top off two cartons and fit the eggs between two bottom pieces and tie them snug, they'll stay put. Takes twice the boxes, but what's the difference? Some people pack eggs in loose oats in lard pails and syrup cans, and tie the lids on tight. Pack your eggs on the top layer in a hard pannier, with heavy, firm cargo on the bottom.

If you use gasoline or kerosene lanterns, a good way to carry the fuel is to put it in *tightly* capped or corked whisky bottles, roll bottles in six or eight thicknesses of newspaper, tie tight and pack upright. Handle all your bottled goods and glass-packed supplies this way. Keep your gas, kerosene, soap, soap powder, etc., away from your food. You'll be happier if you do. I knew two sheepherders who mixed their flour and kerosene in their pack on the way up to camp. When I saw them, their eyes were red from the fumes of biscuits they had eaten for two weeks with the kerosene flour.

Pack gas lanterns and other lanterns in cartons, snug wrapped and upright; radios, cameras, etc., in cartons insulated with burlaps, canvas, or paper. Don't be scotch with the paper. You can look up "help wanted" ads if you don't do this right. Put your cameras, radios, etc., in padded cartons in center of box pannier and surround with soft cargo. Another good place for them is in the center of a bed roll.

When you start loading panniers, use matched pairs together, either hard or soft. Try to put equal weights in each as you go along. Pots, pans, plates, metal ware, kitchen ware, wrapped and padded, pack best in hard panniers. Telescope what you can and fit snug. When you think you're all done, use the scale. Then adjust till weights are equal.

Butter and lard—best to pack tight in a can, wrap this can round and round with paper, put the whole in a larger can, snug and tight. If you take packages, wrap the packages with six or eight thicknesses of paper or cloth and put in tight pail. Fresh meat for your first night out, wrap clean and snug in plastic, paper, and burlap, and pack in hard pannier.

With any pack outfit, if you mantie up your cargo, you need three canvas tarps per load. Call 'em tarps, manties, or pack covers, seven by seven feet square is about right; one tarp for the load on each side, the third for a pack cover. If you use a tent for a top pack, it will replace the pack cover. With panniers instead of mantied loads, you need one pack cover to cover the load on each horse.

Kyacks, alforjas, panniers, or whatever you call 'em may be made of canvas, wood, rawhide, metal, wickerware, willowware, felt, fiberglass plastic, or a combination of these materials. There are a lot of packers on the job in the mountain states of South America, Mexico, western U.S., Canada, and Alaska. Their pouches, bags, sacks, baskets, and boxes, together with their different kinds of pack saddles, and their horses, mules, and burros, all have the same problems and the same mechanical difficulties—different, but still the same.

Some packers use canvas panniers to pack quarters of game or other meat in to camp. Some people mantie the meat to pack it. Lots of others just sling the quarters, hair side to the saddle, throw a pack cover over the whole, and tie down. Because the 2 front quarters weigh about the same, and so do the 2 hind ones, balancing the load is no problem here. Some

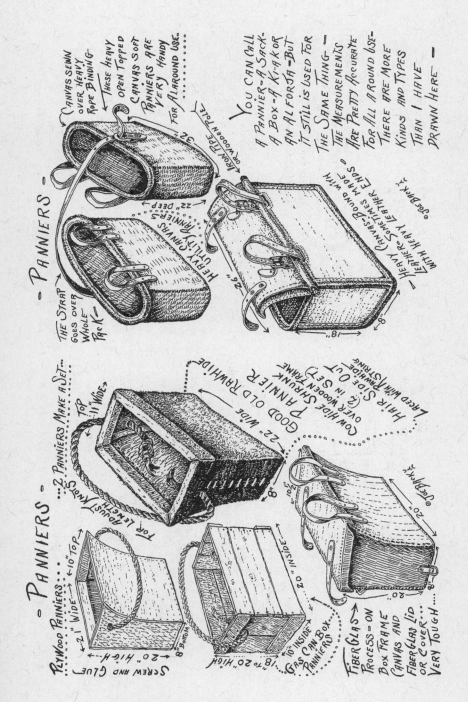

PANNIERS

CANVAS SEWN OVER HEAVY ROPE BINDING ~

THESE HEAVY OPEN TOPPED CANVAS SOFT PANNIERS ARE VERY HANDY FOR A L'AROUND USE.

THE STRAP GOES OVER WHOLE PACK ~

HEAVY CANVAS UTILITY PANNIERS

22" DEEP

26"

32"

IRON TOP POLE OR WOODEN POLE ~

HEAVY CANVAS (SOMETIMES ENDS MADE WITH HEAVY LEATHER ~ SOMETIMES LEATHER ALL AROUND USE ~

8"

18"

You can call A PANNIER — A SACK — A BOX — A KI-AK OR AN ALFORJA — BUT IT STILL IS USED FOR THE SAME THING — THE MEASUREMENTS ARE PRETTY ACCURATE FOR ALL AROUND USE — THERE ARE MORE KINDS AND TYPES THAN I HAVE DRAWN HERE —

PANNIERS

...2 PANNIERS MAKE A SET...

TOP 11" WIDE

22" WIDE

GOOD OLD RAWHIDE PANNIER — COW HIDE SHRUNK OVER A WOODEN FRAME (2 IN SET) HAIR SIDE OUT LACED WITH RAWHIDE (STRING

8"

10½"

20"

8"

PLYWOOD PANNIERS... ← 10" TOP ← 21" WIDE SCREW AND GLUE 20" HIGH 8" BOTTOM

FOR LENGTH ADJUST KNOTS

GAS CAN BOX PANNIERS 10" INSIDE 20" INSIDE 18" TO 20" HIGH

FIBERGLAS → PROCESS — ON BOX FRAME CANVAS AND FIBERGLAS LID OR COVER — VERY TOUGH ...

69

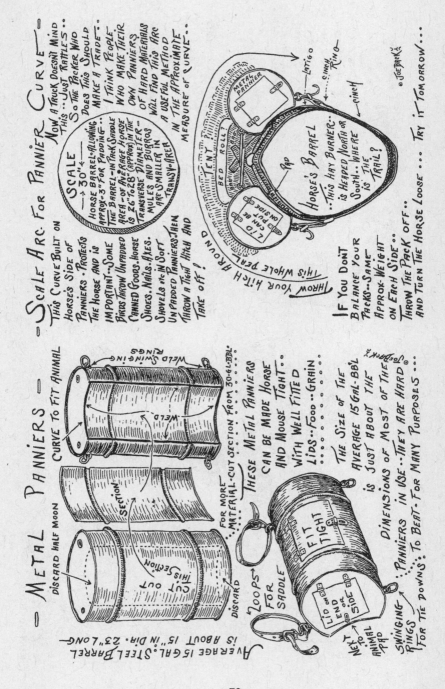

Scale Arc For Pannier Curve

Now a truck doesn't mind this.. just rattles.. so the packer who does this should make a trade.. I think people who make their own panniers of hard materials will find this are a useful method in the approximate measure of curve..

This curve built on horse's side of panniers.. Protects the horse and is important.. Some bikers throw unpadded canned goods, horse shoes, nails, axes, shovels in soft unpadded panniers.. then throw a tight hitch and take off!

SCALE
→ 30" ←
Horse Barrel.. allowing approx. 3" for padding.. the barrel-in pack saddle area-of average horse is 26 to 28 (approx) in the transverse diameter.. mules and burros are smaller in transverse area.

METAL PANNIER — Latigo — cinch ring — cinch — Pap — Bed Roll? — Tent — Lid can be put on side — Horse's Barrel.. this hay burner is heaped north or south.. where is trail?

©Joe Back

Throw your hitch around this whole deal

If you don't balance your packs.. same approx. weight on each side.. throw the pack off.. and turn the horse loose ... try it tomorrow...

Metal Panniers

Curve to fit animal

Weld swinging rings

Discard half moon

Weld

Section

Cut out this section

For more material-cut section from 30-gal.bbl.

These metal panniers can be made horse and mouse tight.. with well fitted lids.. food.. grain

The size of the average 15 gal-bbl is just about the dimensions of most of the panniers in use.. they are hard to beat. For many purposes... for the downs.

Discard

Loops for saddle

Fit tight

Lid on end or side

Next to animal pad

Swinging rings for tie downs

Average 15 gal. Steel Barrel is about 15" in dia. 23" long

©Joe Back

70

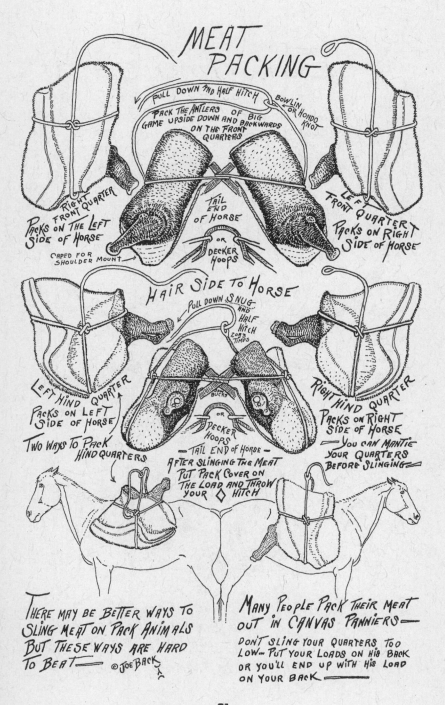

MEAT PACKING

PULL DOWN AND HALF HITCH

BOWLIN OR HONDO KNOT

PACK THE ANTLERS OF BIG GAME UPSIDE DOWN AND BACKWARDS ON THE FRONT QUARTERS

RIGHT FRONT QUARTER PACKS ON THE LEFT SIDE OF HORSE

CAPED FOR SHOULDER MOUNT

TAIL END OF HORSE

OR DECKER HOOPS

LEFT FRONT QUARTER PACKS ON RIGHT SIDE OF HORSE

HAIR SIDE TO HORSE

PULL DOWN SNUG AND HALF HITCH 2 OR 3 TIMES

LEFT HIND QUARTER PACKS ON LEFT SIDE OF HORSE

TWO WAYS TO PACK HIND QUARTERS

BUCKS OR DECKER HOOPS

TAIL END OF HORSE

AFTER SLINGING THE MEAT PUT PACK COVER ON THE LOAD AND THROW YOUR ◇ HITCH

RIGHT HIND QUARTER PACKS ON RIGHT SIDE OF HORSE

YOU CAN MANTIE YOUR QUARTERS BEFORE SLINGING

THERE MAY BE BETTER WAYS TO SLING MEAT ON PACK ANIMALS BUT THESE WAYS ARE HARD TO BEAT —— ©JOE BACK

MANY PEOPLE PACK THEIR MEAT OUT IN CANVAS PANNIERS —

DON'T SLING YOUR QUARTERS TOO LOW— PUT YOUR LOADS ON HIS BACK OR YOU'LL END UP WITH HIS LOAD ON YOUR BACK ——

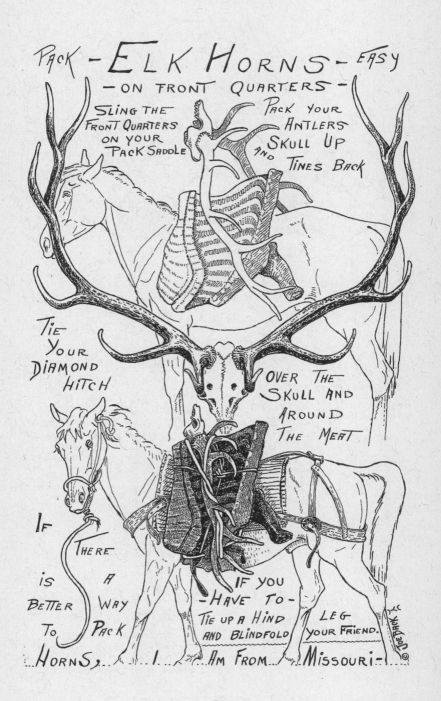

Pack —ELK HORNS— Easy
—ON FRONT QUARTERS—

SLING THE FRONT QUARTERS ON YOUR PACK SADDLE

PACK YOUR ANTLERS SKULL UP AND TINES BACK

TIE YOUR DIAMOND HITCH

OVER THE SKULL AND AROUND THE MEAT

IF THERE IS A BETTER WAY TO PACK HORNS,... I... AM FROM... MISSOURI—

IF YOU —HAVE TO— TIE UP A HIND AND BLINDFOLD LEG YOUR FRIEND.

© JOE BACK

72

···THE BASKET HITCH···
···A SLING···

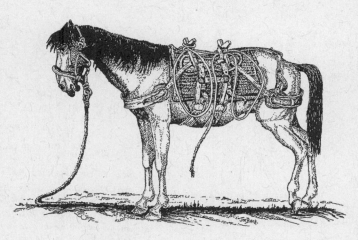

···THE BARREL HITCH···
···A SLING···

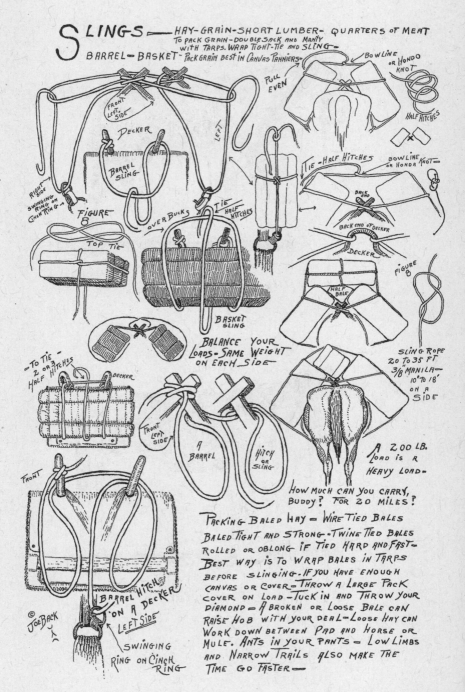

SLINGS — HAY - GRAIN - SHORT LUMBER - QUARTERS OF MEAT

TO PACK GRAIN - DOUBLE SACK AND MANTY
WITH TARPS. WRAP TIGHT - TIE AND SLING -

BARREL - BASKET - PACK GRAIN BEST IN CANVAS PANNIERS-

PULL EVEN

BOWLINE OR HONDO KNOT

HALF HITCHES

FRONT LEFT SIDE

DECKER

LEFT

BARREL SLING

RIGHT SIDE

SWINGING RING ON CINCH RING

FIGURE 8

TIE - HALF HITCHES

BOWLINE OR HONDA KNOT

BACK END

BACK END of DECKER

DECKER

TOP TIE

OVER BUCKS

TIE HALF HITCHES

FIGURE 8

HALF BALE

BASKET SLING

BALANCE YOUR LOADS - SAME WEIGHT ON EACH SIDE

-TO TIE - 2 OR 3 HALF HITCHES

DECKER

FRONT LEFT SIDE

A BARREL

HITCH OR SLING

SLING ROPE 20 TO 35 FT 3/8 MANILA - 10' TO 18' ON A SIDE

A 200 LB. LOAD IS A HEAVY LOAD -

FRONT

HOW MUCH CAN YOU CARRY, BUDDY? FOR 20 MILES!

BARREL HITCH ON A DECKER LEFT SIDE

© JOE BACK

SWINGING RING ON CINCH RING

PACKING BALED HAY - WIRE TIED BALES
BALED TIGHT AND STRONG - TWINE TIED BALES
ROLLED OR OBLONG - IF TIED HARD AND FAST -
BEST WAY IS TO WRAP BALES IN TARPS
BEFORE SLINGING - IF YOU HAVE ENOUGH
CANVAS OR COVER - THROW A LARGE PACK
COVER ON LOAD - TUCK IN AND THROW YOUR
DIAMOND - A BROKEN OR LOOSE BALE CAN
RAISE HOB WITH YOUR DEAL - LOOSE HAY CAN
WORK DOWN BETWEEN PAD AND HORSE OR
MULE. ANTS IN YOUR PANTS — LOW LIMBS
AND NARROW TRAILS ALSO MAKE THE
TIME GO FASTER —

···· Some Ways To Do It ····

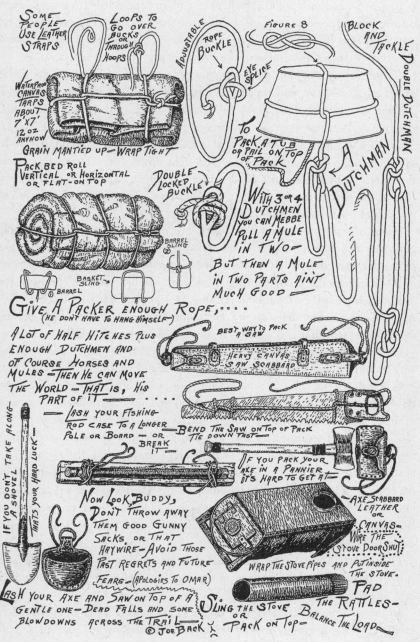

Some People Use Leather Straps

Loops To Go Over Bucks or Through Hoops

Adjustable Rope Buckle

Figure 8

Eye Splice

Block And Tackle

Double Dutchman

Waterproof Canvas Tarps About 7'x7' 12 oz anyhow

To Pack A Tub or Pail on Top of Pack

A Dutchman

Grain Mantied Up—Wrap Tight

Pack Bed Roll Vertical or Horizontal or Flat—on Top

Double Locked Buckle

With 3 or 4 Dutchmen you can mebbe Pull A Mule in Two—

But Then A Mule in Two Parts Ain't Much Good—

Barrel Sling

Basket Sling

Barrel

Give A Packer Enough Rope,····
(He Don't Have To Hang Himself)

A Lot of Half Hitches Plus Enough Dutchmen and Of Course Horses and Mules—Then He Can Move The World—That Is, His Part Of It····

Best Way To Pack A Saw

Heavy Canvas Saw Scabbard

— Lash Your Fishing Rod Case To A Longer Pole or Board — or Break It

Bend The Saw On Top of Pack Tie Down Fast—

If You Pack Your Axe In A Pannier It's Hard To Get At—

If You Don't Take Along—A Shovel Your Hard Luck—

That's Your Hard Luck—

Now Look Buddy, Don't Throw Away Them Good Gunny Sacks or That Haywire—Avoid Those Past Regrets and Future Fears—(Apologies To Omar)

— Axe Scabbard Leather or Canvas—

Wire The Stove Door Shut—

Wrap The Stove Pipes and Put Inside The Stove.

Lash Your Axe and Saw on Top of A Gentle One—Dead Falls and Some Blowdowns Across The Trail
© Joe Back

Sling The Stove or Pack On Top—

Pad The Rattles— Balance The Load—

75

men who hunt the way-back country bone their meat. Anyone with a little experience can bone an elk in little over an hour and not leave enough meat on the bones to make soup. Put the meat from each side in a clean meat sack, put one sack in each of a pair of panniers, the hide goes on like a pack cover, then the horns and the diamond and you are set to go.

Large trophy size horns or antlers are not hard to pack. If you have killed a bull elk, say, and caped him out, sling the front quarters on a pack animal. On top of them place the antlers, upside down and backwards, nose of skull in the air, tines down and pointed toward the animal's rear. The average large elk head (set of antlers) usually has about the right spread so that when the antlers are brought down over the meat pack on the average horse, they just about make a good fit. The last two tines are just about even with the cinch rings, or lower. Throw a good diamond hitch over all this, and you're off.

Sacks of oats, or grain of any sort, are either packed in large canvas panniers or are mantied up in canvas and slung on a pack saddle. Take particular care that the two sides, weighing equal, are slung at the same level—the same distance down from the pack saddle. Do this carefully for every pack—whether it is panniers, mantied grain, baled hay, tents, bedrolls, lumber, boxes, bales of any sort, chain saws, machinery, light plants, or anything else that is divided into two equal parts and weight.

If you are packing ore, or any unyielding object, in canvas panniers, be sure you have plenty padding to insulate same and protect the pack animal.

Going down the trail, once in a while the pack outfit comes to a big tree down, or maybe three or four blowdowns and deadfalls there is no way around. Dadburn it, you've just got to stop and saw your way through. Hell's bells, you wrapped up that axe and put it in a box pannier on that big black away back at the end of the string! Saw's back there, too. The best place to pack an axe, I think, is lashed tight on top of a pack, with the head in a scabbard with a tie-down on it. Then you can get to it in a hurry. Have a heavy scabbard (canvas is good) for your cross-cut saw. Bend the saw, in its scabbard, across the outside middle of a pack and lash down tight. You may need it bad.

Pack your shovel blade in a scabbard, or wrap snug with burlap and canvas and tie. You can pack it on top, on the outside of a pack, or put it in a pannier, handle up and back.

If you like the gadget and have one, a chain saw is faster than the other kind. It takes up twenty-five or thirty pounds, and some space in a pannier, which isn't hard to rig. A top pack is handier, if you figure out an easy system to protect it, and lash it tight. Any top pack has to be balanced with side packs, and must be as flat and low down as possible.

If you are in a bind, and have to pack anything on a riding saddle, handle the deal just about the way you would a pack saddle. The horn is used as the front buck, and the cantle as the back buck. In the middle of a twenty-five or thirty foot rope throw a couple of half hitches, and tighten them on the horn, with half the rope on each side of the horse. Throw each end, right and left, around the cantle and back over the seat, just like the sling on the pack saddle in my illustration. Tie the short jockey string and the longer flank skirt strings together, over the rope, in a square knot. They will hold the sling rope from sliding back over the curve of the cantle. You can pack most anything, using this sling as your base, on a riding saddle.

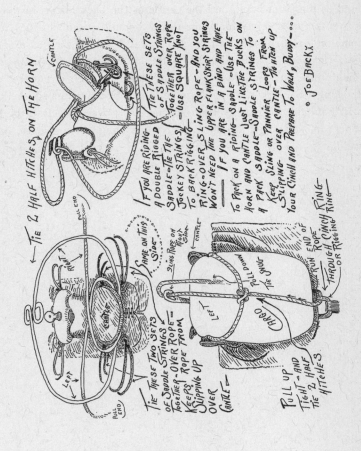

·.· To Sling and Pack on A Riding Saddle ·.·

← Tie 2 half hitches on the horn

Cantle

If you are riding a double rigged saddle—tie the jockey strings to back rigging—

Tie these sets of saddle strings together over rope —use square knot—

Over sling rope—and you won't need the upper flank skirt strings

If you are in a bind and have no back rigging

To pack on a riding saddle—use the horn and cantle just like the bucks on a pack saddle—saddle strings to keep sling or pannier loops from slipping over cantle—tighten up your cinch and prepare to walk, Buddy—·.·

© Joe Back ×

Tie these two sets of saddle strings together—over rope—keeps rope from slipping up over cantle—

Right

Left

Pull end

Same on this side

Sling rope on right side

Cantle

Pull end

Pull up tight—and tie the 2 half hitches

Left

Pull down

Tie spur

Argo

Run end of rope through cinch ring or rigging ring—

FINISHING HITCHES AND FINAL TIES

Now that all the hard work is done: the pads, saddle, and load in place, the load looped, slung, or stuck on, and (there it goes again) balanced; the only thing left to do is to make sure the load stays in place and does not shift in any way.

About this time, if you are built long you'll have it easier, and if you are short you'll wish you was long. But the long and short of it is that good packers come in all sizes.

A few people have rigged sort of a cargo net of rope, spliced or tied, to hold the load in place. I've seen very few. Some seem to work fairly well. This net, about thirty-six inches square, is thrown over the top and droops down over the sides and ends of the horse's pack. A dutchman (see illustrations) is then anchored to a cinch ring on either side and pulled snug and tight, just as a trucker throws a net over his load in the truck and anchors all four corners.

Now, everybody has a right to his own opinion and can pack his own way, but to me that is the poorest and most impractical hitch that can be devised: you can't keep it tight. The sides and ends of a truck box are fairly rigid, and do not have a sweating and shrinking to loosen the net up, unless it's the driver in the cab who's worried about his load.

I've heard a few people say there are better ways to put a final tie on a load than with a diamond hitch. Sometimes you can get along without it, but most of the time I disagree. Say, you're packing a lot of identical items, easy to sling, loop, or hitch to the bucks, loops, or horn of a saddle. If you're traveling very slowly, a relatively short distance, with plumb gentle or dead-head horses, lots of times just a barrel or basket hitch or even a gilligan hitch will hold the load—and that is no hitch at all. A couple of dutchmen tied in the right way and with discretion will also do the trick. Even then, it's quicker, handier, safer, and more practical to use one of several good diamond hitches.

From the standpoint of what the cargo is, the fact is that there's a big difference between packing diversified items in odd-sized packages and weights, rolled, mantied, or wrapped, on one horse; and packing say two

···THE LONG OF IT···

···THE SHORT OF IT···

quarters of meat, baled hay, lumber, salt in blocks or 100-pound sacks, or other items of uniform weight and bulk so as to twin up on the sides of the pack animal.

Whatever the cargo, when you use a diamond there is safety first in the first step. No matter what kind of diamond, you first throw over and around the pack horse a rope and lash cinch to secure the load to the horse. This may be Greek to you at first, but after a few trips when you do all the work, you'll sure see the point.

When people discard the use of the diamond hitch, or don't use a lash cinch and lash rope to make a final tie on a load on a pack animal, the only way to hold the sides of packed cargo securely and flop proof depends on fastening the load to the *saddle* rather than to the *horse*. You use a block and tackle principle, passing a rope or ropes through the cinch rings and/ or the rigging rings of the pack saddle, or maybe the riding saddle. This works fine to a certain degree, and is practical for some styles and kinds of loads. Most every packer does this sometimes and for varied reasons. But when you don't add a lash cinch and rope to end in a diamond hitch or its equivalent, here is what happens:

When a saddle is cinched on a horse, it is just about like clamping a pair of pants on that animal we are most familiar with, homo sap. The double or single cinch goes around and clings to the horse's barrel from the sternum or breastbone on up the sides, and still slings from the latigoes in the cinch rings to the rigging rings and saddle tree, all the way to the back-bone. This means that any kind of saddle on an animal is in very close contact all the way round, via cinch, latigoes, blankets, rigging rings, and saddle tree. That is what keeps the load on, as we all know, including the encircled and surrounded hay burner. We are depending on friction and gravity.

When you put a load on a saddled animal, and then secure the top and sides of it to the cinch rings (or even higher, to the rigging rings), with various rope arrangements drawn tight and tied, you are pulling the latigoes and the upper parts of the cinchas away and *out* from his body. Now the only thing holding the load on is the area of cinch or cinchas, saddle, blanket, and latigo, that still touches the horse's body. Take a gander. There's a big gap that you can see, in the frictional value of the cinched saddle on this horse.

And here, let me point out, lays the reason many times, if this system is followed on trip after trip, for sternum and belly sores, and pies and sores on the back of this unlucky animal.

I have seen a pack horse, and so have countless other packers, who came safely into camp with his saddle cinchas plenty loose, maybe because of shrinkage, packer's lack of skill, or just plain happenstance. Why he hadn't lost his pack was that it was balanced good and had an A-1 and tight diamond hitch over the whole load. The wide lash cinch around the horse's chest was the only belt still tight and snug. An A-1 diamond on the pack animal is what lots of times saves trouble, time, and flesh of man and beast.

The function of cinch or cinchas on saddle, plus billet straps and latigoes, is to firmly and snugly attach and keep said saddle on an animal where it'll do the most good. So, when you secure the pack by the aid of cinch rings rather than by extra cinch and rope arrangement, you destroy a lot of horse and pack health insurance.

If you have learned to tie those pretty bows in your shoe strings—and they are intricate—you can sure as manila learn to throw a diamond hitch on a packed animal, and throw it right. It's no more complicated. You can tie or untie your shoes in the dark. When you tie and untie the diamond hitch as often as you do your shoestrings you'll have to agree with me.

Manila is the stuff. Most people, including me, like good manila rope for both pack and sling ropes (sling ropes 3/8 inch diameter, lash ropes 5/8 or sometimes 3/4 inch diameter: a good many times you will use a lash rope also for a picket rope, and will want it big for safety). Of course, you can use sisal, which is cheaper, and I think much weaker and less durable than manila. Cotton is good, but boy! when she gets wet and frozen you need a hacksaw blade for your knots. Nylon is a billionaire's dream, and say, Bud, try to splice one! Besides, you've seen the ads praising the stretch in milady's nylons; it's so, it never stops, you can't keep it tight. Good, A-1 manila hemp is hard to beat: strong, wears well, splices easy when worn or broken, and for all-around work is the best. When manila gets wet and freezes, knots and hitches are not for lily fingers to fiddle with either; but take it as it comes, I'll stick to manila.

For length, use about forty to forty-five feet for lash ropes, about thirty-five on sling ropes—that gives you plenty. If you short yourself, you'll be sorry.

I have illustrated many ways and means of securing various loads to the pack saddle before throwing the final hitch, and about five or six different kinds of diamond hitches. Most of these have been used by packers for many years. There are without doubt many other ways to do these things, but you'll have to ask the other fellow about them. These are the ones I know about, and I've found them hard to beat. Follow the drawings and the diagrams, and you can tie these hitches. Some are tied better by two men, but all can be tied by one man, if he has to.

All these diamonds have one thing in common, they help to hold up the panniers, rolls, bales, quarters of meat, or mantied cargo, to more even balance; because part of the hitch, on both sides of the load, goes under to support it, besides clamping and enclosing it in a Hollywood embrace. Besides this, the lash cinch helps and insures the whole deal, as you can see by all the pack horse illustrations. The diamond is a custom-built cargo net without the net's weaknesses.

All these diamond hitches are started by first throwing a lash cinch across the horse's load. This cinch has a ring at one end and a hook at the other, and to the ring is attached the lash rope, forty to forty-five feet long: a double diamond takes four to six feet more rope than a single does. The hook is to help tie quicker and unpack faster—you can use a cinch with a ring in each end when you have to. A lash cinch is usually wider and six to eight inches longer than a saddle cinch.

To simplify the directions in the diagrams, I did not specify, except on the first one, that the first thing most packers do when starting to throw almost any diamond hitch, is to place the "jerk end," or last part of the rope, along the top of the pack lengthwise with the knot below the pony's tail, *then* throw the lash cinch with the other end of the rope tied to it, over the middle of the pack, catch the hook, and proceed to the diamond. This one operation sometimes confuses the new operator for the first time.

The main thing about tieing a diamond of any type is, after the lash cinch and rope are thrown over the center of the pack, catch and hook the rope, and *pull down snug right now.* When you twist and pull to tie the diamond hitch, the rope is bound to loosen somewhat, but the principle remains, *once you start, never give slack.* If you throw over the pack and catch the hook and don't pull snug right then, the folds of the canvas pack cover (or whatever your top pack is) will trap you into pulling sideways when you come to jerking down the final tie. Same problem as tieing a stout string on a package wrapped tight for shipping to Cousin Willy in Timbuctoo.

I have drawn six diamond hitches for this book, and made a drawing

83

TIE YOUR OWN DIAMOND HITCH

JIM BRIDGER USED IT

NO. 2

NO. 1

NO. 3

NO.7 START HERE: LAY THIS END OF LOOP BACK OF RIGHT PANNIER, THEN UNDER IT.

RIGHT SIDE UNDER PACK

KEEP THIS ROPE PLENTY TIGHT AS YOU GO AROUND. NEVER LET GO

No.7

RING END OF LASH CINCH TO FRONT UNDERNEATH

TAIL END OF HORSE

JERK ROPE TIGHT FOR FINAL TIE

WRAP THIS LOOP TWICE UNDER ROPE JUST BELOW IT

NO. 4

LASH ROPE ON TOP OF PACK

END

ROPE UNDER PACK LEFT SIDE

PACK COVER

PANNIER

HOOK END OF LASH CINCH TO LEFT SIDE UNDERNEATH

JERK ROPE TIGHT FOR FINAL TIE

NO. 5

LASH ROPE END ON TOP OF PACK

SIDE END

PULL UP THROUGH LOOP

RIGHT SIDE

HEAD END OF HORSE

TOP OF PACK

No.8 TOP VIEW DIAMOND HITCH ALL TIED

TAIL END OF HORSE

ROPE TO JERK FOR FINAL TIE

NO. 6

LOOP FOR RIGHT SIDE OF PACK

FINAL TIE JERK ROPE

LOOP FOR LEFT SIDE OF PACK

LEFT SIDE HOOK END

LEFT SIDE

PACK COVER

BOX PANNIER

FINAL TIE: TWO HALF HITCHES ON LEFT SIDE UNDER PACK

© JOE W. BACK 1948

84

DOUBLE DIAMOND HITCH

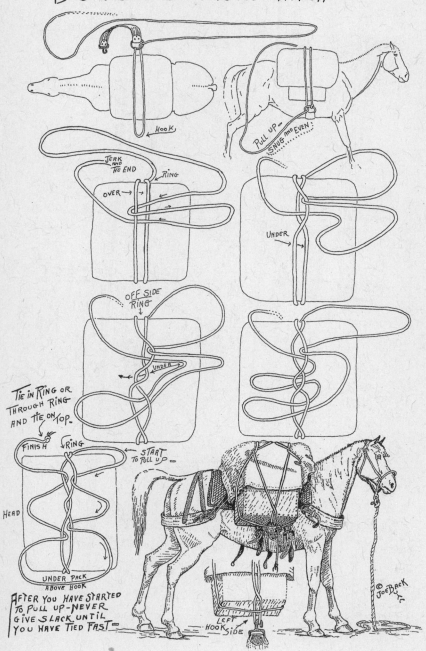

HOOK

PULL UP

SNUG AND EVEN

JERK AND TIE END

RING

OVER

UNDER

OFF SIDE RING

UNDER

TIE IN RING OR
THROUGH RING
AND TIE ON TOP.

FINISH

RING

START TO PULL UP

HEAD

UNDER PACK ABOVE HOOK

AFTER YOU HAVE STARTED
TO PULL UP—NEVER
GIVE SLACK UNTIL
YOU HAVE TIED FAST—

LEFT HOOK SIDE

© JOE BACK JC

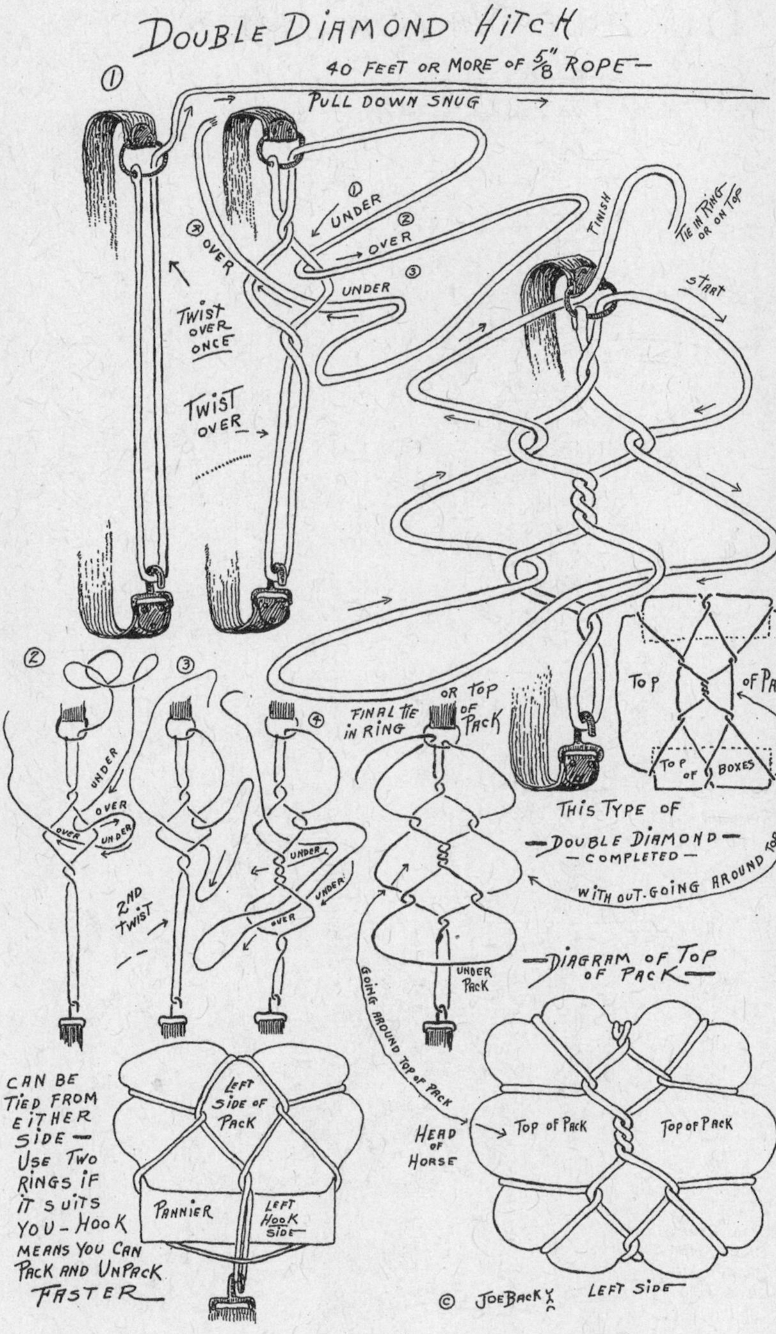

DOUBLE DIAMOND HITCH

40 FEET OR MORE OF 5/8" ROPE —

① PULL DOWN SNUG

③ OVER

① UNDER
② OVER
③ UNDER

TWIST OVER ONCE

TWIST OVER

FINISH

TIE IN RING OR ON TOP

START

② UNDER OVER UNDER

③ 2ND TWIST

④ UNDER OVER UNDER

FINAL TIE IN RING OR TOP OF PACK

TOP OF PACK

OF PACK

TOP OF BOXES

THIS TYPE OF
— DOUBLE DIAMOND —
— COMPLETED —
WITH OUT. GOING AROUND TOP OF PACK

GOING AROUND TOP OF PACK

UNDER PACK

— DIAGRAM OF TOP OF PACK —

CAN BE TIED FROM EITHER SIDE — USE TWO RINGS IF IT SUITS YOU — HOOK MEANS YOU CAN PACK AND UNPACK FASTER

LEFT SIDE OF PACK

PANNIER

LEFT HOOK SIDE

HEAD OF HORSE

TOP OF PACK

TOP OF PACK

© JOE BACK

LEFT SIDE

86

—ONE MAN DIAMOND— TWO IS BETTER

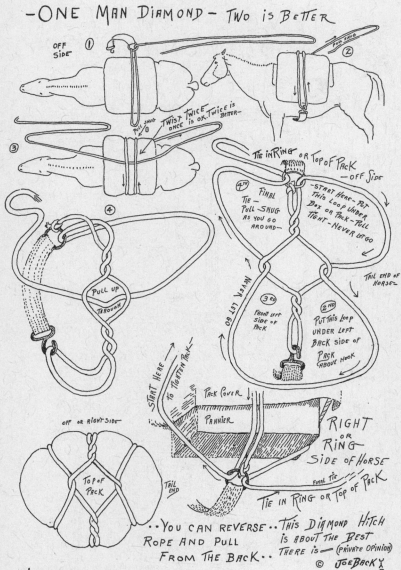

OFF SIDE ①

② PULL SNUG

PULL SNUG ③

TWIST TWICE — ONCE IS OK, TWICE IS BETTER—

④ PULL UP THROUGH

TIE IN RING or TOP OF PACK — OFF SIDE

④TH FINAL TIE — PULL SNUG AS YOU GO AROUND—

—START HERE— PUT THIS LOOP UNDER BOX OR PACK—PULL TIGHT—NEVER LET GO

TAIL END OF HORSE

NEVER LET GO

③RD FRONT LEFT SIDE OF PACK

②ND PUT THIS LOOP UNDER LEFT BACK SIDE OF PACK ABOVE HOOK

START HERE —TO TIGHTEN PACK—

PACK COVER ↓

PANNIER

RIGHT OR RING SIDE OF HORSE

OFF OR RIGHT SIDE—

TOP OF PACK

TAIL END

FINAL TIE

TIE IN RING OR TOP OF PACK

··YOU CAN REVERSE·· ROPE AND PULL FROM THE BACK··

··THIS DIAMOND HITCH IS ABOUT THE BEST THERE IS — (PRIVATE OPINION)
© JOE BACK

·· IF YOUR HORSE GETS TOUGH —TIE A HIND LEG UP AND BLINDFOLD HIM ··

87

NEVER SWEAT
DIAMOND — FAST AND EASY —
HITCH
SINGLE OR DOUBLE

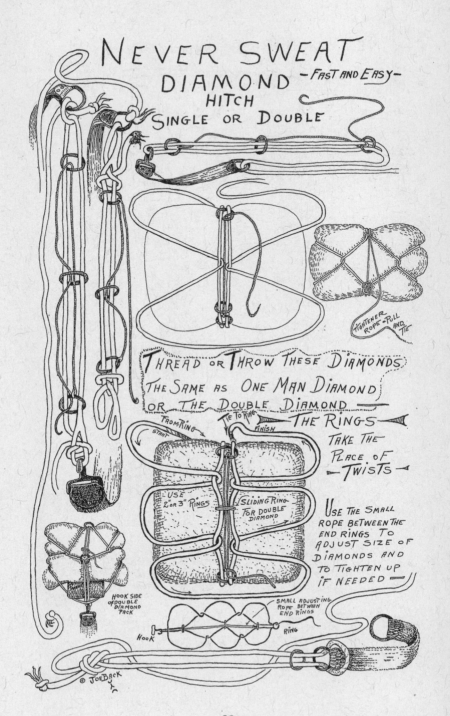

THREAD or THROW THESE DIAMONDS
THE SAME AS ONE MAN DIAMOND
OR THE DOUBLE DIAMOND —

THE RINGS —
TAKE THE
PLACE OF
TWISTS ◄

USE THE SMALL
ROPE BETWEEN THE
END RINGS TO
ADJUST SIZE OF
DIAMONDS AND
TO TIGHTEN UP
IF NEEDED —

TIGHTENER ROPE - PULL AND TIE

FROM RING
START
TIE TO RING
FINISH

USE 2 OR 3" RINGS

SLIDING RING FOR DOUBLE DIAMOND

HOOK SIDE OF DOUBLE DIAMOND PACK

SMALL ADJUSTING ROPE BETWEEN END RINGS

HOOK

RING

© JOE BACK

Box Hitch with Half Hitched Diamond

CAN BE USED WITH OUT HALF HITCHES ON BOXES
THERE IS, OF COURSE, LOTS OF OTHER WAYS
TO DO THIS—
(PANNIERS)
(ALFORJAS)

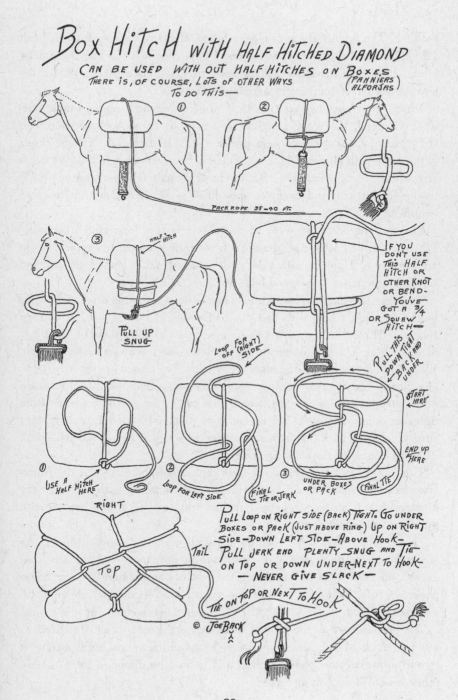

PACK ROPE 35-40 FT.

HALF HITCH

PULL UP SNUG

IF YOU DON'T USE THIS HALF HITCH OR OTHER KNOT OR BEND—YOU'VE GOT A ¾ OR SQUAW HITCH—

PULL THIS DOWN TIGHT BACK AND UNDER

LOOP FOR OFF (RIGHT) SIDE

START HERE

END UP HERE

① USE A HALF HITCH HERE

② LOOP FOR LEFT SIDE

FINAL TIE OR JERK

③ UNDER BOXES OR PACK

FINAL TIE

RIGHT

TOP

TAIL

PULL LOOP ON RIGHT SIDE (BACK) TIGHT. GO UNDER BOXES OR PACK (JUST ABOVE RING) UP ON RIGHT SIDE—DOWN LEFT SIDE—ABOVE HOOK—PULL JERK END PLENTY SNUG AND TIE ON TOP OR DOWN UNDER—NEXT TO HOOK— NEVER GIVE SLACK—

TIE ON TOP OR NEXT TO HOOK

© JOE BACK

89

entitled "The Squaw Hitch." I have heard of many "squaw hitches," but I'll bet you agree with me that the one I have drawn is the one real squaw hitch. Its simple directness leaves most compassionate people with a desire for a slightly humane if less simple diamond.

I have illustrated two ways to tie a double diamond, one a simple one-twist diamond, the other a tighter two-twist diamond, both double. On some varied loads some packers prefer a double diamond. The principle is the same with all these diamond hitches. You can tie a 6-diamond hitch if you want to, or even more. But the more diamonds you tie on one pack, the longer it takes; and the extra ones do no good. You won't get to camp so quick.

For me, the best and most practical one is the "one man diamond." When it can be beat for all practical loads in any country, weather, or on any animal, I'll put in with you. Suit yourself, take your choice, if you can find any better ones, good luck and have at it!

The diamond that can be used as a single or as a double diamond I have used a lot. It's a help with this one to be able to do a good job of rope splicing. Three 3-inch or 3½-inch diameter iron rings and six or eight feet of ¼-inch or 3/8 inch diameter for tightener, and you can do a real job. With this "never sweat diamond hitch" you don't need to throw a twist any place. The rings do the job. *And,* after you are on the trail, and some horse shrinks and his cinchas loosen, just catch him and pull on the little tightener rope. This pulls the diamond or diamonds smaller, and tightens your cinch and pack. Jerk this tightener rope down tight, and half-hitch its end a couple of times, and you're off.

This "never sweat diamond" is the simplest one there is. But the funny (not ha! ha!) part of it is, you'd better pack a while with the ordinary diamond hitch in order to know how and why, and *what you can do* with the never sweat diamond.

The so-called "box hitch" can be tied with most any diamond hitch. As you can see in the drawing, it's just half-hitching panniers (or any side packs) on both sides before tieing the rest of the diamond hitch. Some packers figure this half-hitch addition gives a kind of double indemnity to a packer's policy. It helps a lot, even if it does cost the boss for more rope.

The principle of all the hitches is a tie that tightens in all directions as you pull the final end. But if you haven't packed the animal right, balanced it, and adjusted your pads, cinchas, and saddle, no diamond hitch or any other kind will do you any good.

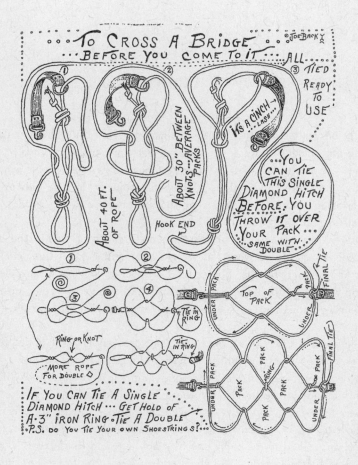

Pardner, if you *have* got your pads, pack, and cinchas like they oughta be, here's a diamond hitch *you oughta know about,* if you don't. You can "Cross a bridge before you come to it" with this one. Look at my drawing and figure it out. No twists, just two knots; like the "never sweat diamond" in a way. It's a good one. You can tie it *before* you put it over a pack. When you unpack, just unhook, and it's ready to adjust for the next time you pack. There is other ways to pre-tie diamonds, but you can't beat this one. And, Buddy, if you want to put the ring end of lash cinch where the drawing says "hook loop," you can throw the lash cinch and pre-tied diamond over the pack and tie the *other* way round. Bud, you'll like this diamond hitch!

91

ROPE SHORTAGE—REPAIRS AND MAKESHIFTS

It might be well at this turn of the trail to gossip a little about makeshift repairs, and make do things you can fall back on, and may have to. Lots of times you find yourself with your britchen down and wonder where in Hellifax that there rope got to. Mebbe that rope is the one you or some other hoosier lost off his saddle when that packhorse got bogged down and you had to pull him out.

Many fellows have found out that when they've been out in the hills a long time, ropes plumb wear out, or get lost; and besides that, packs get bigger and bulkier, because ponies have strayed or got lost or crippled up, and you've had to double up on the packs; and you've got game meat and didn't bring enough extra lash and sling rope to bring home the—ah—bacon.

When some hard-working bird packs a horse and is just about to pull the jerk end of rope and finds he hasn't enough to hardly, and *I mean hardly*, come through his last diamond loop, he suddenly feels like the sheriff had done foreclosed. All those horses packed, snowing, cold, a long way to go, and *boots on*—not even shoe laces to help out, everything else packed. The only thing to do is take the halter rope off the horse he's working on, to add to the *short end* he's holding, and *dadburn it, it's slipping!* And boy, has he got the short end of it all, the horse he's packing can't be trusted with his halter rope gone. He's got a hind leg tied up already, as he's a spooky bronc. The *only* rope he's got *extry* is the rope he hung on the bronc's shoulders and on down to the hind leg that's up. Now, my valued and bug-eyed friend, don't laugh! Wait'll this kind of comedy lands on your pretty carcass.

What would you do, my grinning friend? Well, don't just stand there, just give me that good fancy leather belt you've got on that pot belly and we'll get this over in a hurry. Use mine? Why, you talk like a silly old woman, man, I done cut mine in two to pack them other two short-rope nags.

Now, buddy, if you think that the above don't happen, you are just in

92

the first grade and that is just a deelicious sample of the first course. There is a lot of funny ha ha jokes, and there is a lot that ain't so ha ha.

When you know beforehand that you are short on rope, you can help out, though it weakens, by untwisting one strand (rope is usually three-strand) off of several good ropes, and twisting up two-strand ropes from the sad orphans you've made. Sometimes you have to rob Peter to pay Paul. Don't do this too often or you will cause the outfit to go broke.

So it pays to figure ahead and allow for this and that, that might, and could, happen. I have seen outfits come in after long trips (and it's happened to me) with very little halter rope left, and pack ropes eked out with strings cut from fresh game hide, long strips of twisted canvas (probably from old tents, but where did that extra pair of drawers go to?) and hay-wire. That is where outfits get the titles, onery and not honorary, of hay-wire and shirt tail!

To help out in a rope shortage you sure need to be able to tie knots and to splice rope. Anybody can or should be able to tie knots—no slip knots. God forbid that a slip knot be used in any way for any purpose on a horse's or a human's body (except maybe on the neck of horse thieves!). An old country Scotsman must have invented the splice; it's a great rope saver, and a time and life saver as well. You don't have to be one of these intellectual monstrosities to do it. A hell of a lot of illiterates can splice, and do. All you have to do is just want to.

As for repairs, out of rope and burlap and canvas you can make stirrups, halters, bridles, quirts; rerig saddles; make block and tackles; cinchas, latigoes, splint bindings, hobbles, breast collars, britchen, pannier repairs, tent repairs, and a lot of other useful items for a horse outfit. Keep whang leather strings, snaps and odd rings, along with stout needles, thread, and beeswax in your repair outfit. But the best thing is to start out with a good, strong, clean, serviceable outfit.

One of the handiest and most practical uses of a rope for riding or packing is the rope hackamore. There are lots of terms and uses for what is after all just a rope on a horse's head and sometimes in his mouth. There are lots of ways to do it, too. Whatever you may call it, I think you'll find this one of use many times. It was shown and taught to me more than forty years ago, and, like many other people, I have found it to be good. It can also be adapted to use in the pony's mouth; but that's usually hard on him, and generally needless. Lots of hands have had to use their hard twist

93

A Rope Hackamore

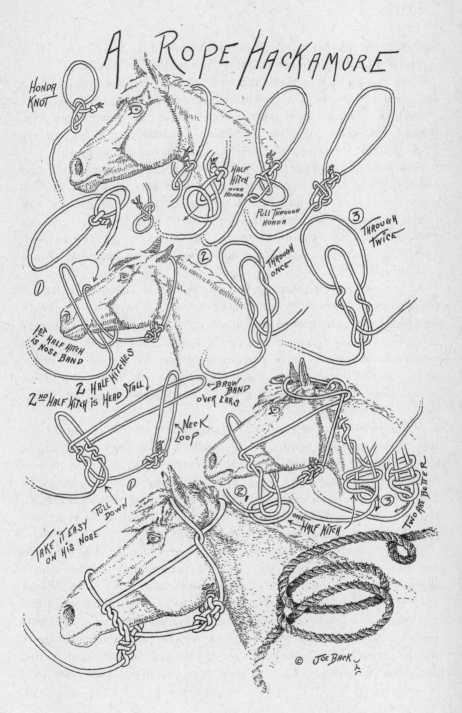

Honda Knot

Half Hitch over honda

Pull through honda

1

2 Through once

3 Through twice

1st Half Hitch is Nose Band

2 Half Hitches

2nd Half Hitch is Head Stall

Brow Band over ears

Neck Loop

Take 'it easy Pull down on his nose

1

2 One Half Hitch

3 Two are better

© Joe Back

94

saddle ropes for this hackamore, and it works OK; but the best to use is a soft dry rope, 5/8 or ½ inch in diameter.

If you can tie a shoe string, you can tie this one from my drawing.

Many people, who have killed a deer while out hunting horseback, just throw it across the saddle and balance it the best they can; then take a rope and tie into a cinch ring or rigging ring, half-hitch the head or tail end, then throw the rest of the rope over and half-hitch the other end to the opposite ring. Of course, the best way is to get a pack horse to the deer, quarter it up, and pack it in easy; but usually it saves time to throw it on the saddle horse and bring it in to camp in one trip. If it is a big buck, sometimes the horns can cause plenty grief. Lots of birds riding a strong, gentle horse just throw it on the saddle, hop on behind the cantle, and ride into camp in style. But lots of times, trying to do this with large deer and on some horses is more painful than stylish.

Sometimes a fellow kills an elk, moose, or some other animal too big to put on a horse. Perhaps he doesn't have pack horses, or the weather looks bad, and anyway for some reason he thinks two trips are out; then he has to figure on taking this piece of good luck to camp right now, somehow. A travois is a good way to do this, and it has been done thousands of times. Look at the years the old Indian gal did most of her hauling that way. It sure pays to keep a good hunting axe or hatchet on your saddle, for this is hard to do with a jacknife. Get two long trimmed green or dry poles, 16 feet or longer, and about 2 inches in diameter at the top. Lash them in an X at your saddlehorn with half-hitches and wraps. With a pole on each side of your horse, tie and lash another pole about 3 feet long to and between the travois poles. Lash a longer one or two below this one as a platform to tie your game carcass to. A lot of rough country can be traveled over in this way without bruising your meat. Quarter-inch rope is good for this deal.

Some hunters leave the hide connected on a pair of front quarters or a pair of hind quarters on an elk, cut a hole in front middle of hide, and throw them over the saddle so that the horn goes through the hole, and there's a quarter on each side. Then half-hitch to the cinch ring, on each side, and start walking. That way you've got half your meat in on the first trip; and if you don't mind walking, and if you give the pony a rest and feed between times, you can get the second half in the same way, without a pack horse.

ON THE TRAIL

Now you're all packed up and ready to go. What'll you do, turn the ponies loose or tail them together?

On good trails with few down trees and with shallow streams, you can make better time by leading your pack string, either tailed together or by tieing each one to the back buck or hoop of the pack saddle ahead. If possible, tail no more than three or four horses together, with one man to lead each set. If you don't want to tail horses together, tie the lead rope to the back buck of the pack saddle of the horse ahead. Use ¼-inch rope or double thickness of hay bale twine. A led balky horse, or a horse in a jackpot, will break this string with no damage to him or to the leading horse. Or you can half-hitch a ring to the leading horse's tail, then tie the lead rope of the horse behind to weak ¼-inch rope and then to ring, so it will break in a bind or jackpot. Nobody hurt—just catch horse and re-tie. Tie the led horse far enough away from the leading horse so he can't be kicked; and still not too long, so led horse can't step over the lead rope and get tangled up.

In case some wild and wooly bird gets in a hurry, and ties a led horse to the sling rope, cargo rope, or diamond hitch rope, or anywhere to the pack itself, he is going to raise hob with the outfit. If a poorly halter-broke horse rares back, or if the led horse spooks, he may jerk the leading horse down, or jerk his pack half off. Leading a horse by the pack saddle is OK, but the surest way is to tail.

On bad trails, across deep streams, bog holes, slide rock, and along canyon trails, it's safer to drive the pack horses loose, and let them pick their own way around bad and chancy sections. A lot of the time the pack animal shows far better judgment than the packer. (Wire nose-baskets on the halters stop eating on the go.) Two-legged fools rush in where four-legged angels fear to tread.

The don't-give-a-damn, hell-on-wheels, suicide type of packer is the gent who rides along leading a horse (Buddie, he don't have to be packed and he can even be a mule) with the lead rope *tied* hard and fast, or with a loop, around his saddle horn. The led animal may spook, or step on a

....TAILING UP....

Meat horses tailed.

Tied wrong and in trouble.

Let 'em pick their own way.

Suicide type packer—tied to saddle horn.

Riding a wring-tail—no time to roll a smoke.

snapping stick and jump. *Don't you do this.* Take a dally or two around the horn. (A dally is a turn or a wrap.) Don't use a loop or tie half-hitches on the horn. A dally or two you can let slip, but if you tie hard and fast or use a loop you are starting a conversation with St. Peter. Mebbe a bear rears up in front of your horse. If you can't turn loose in a hurry, mebbe you'll end up in the bear. Again, your horse may get the lead-rope under his tail. You'll then be in no position to roll a smoke. Mebbe you'd gone to sleep. Mebbe your saddle-horse is a wringtail—one of those nervous boys that's always flopping his tail around, then gets scared to death if he catches something with it. Mebbe it's just your time to meet the man with the scythe. Mebbe! Buddy, that horn was built into your saddle for a lot of good uses, but you can make it Gabriel's horn!

When you tail or tie horses together, be sure they are friends, or at least tolerate each other. If you are riding a pony who hates the one you are leading, or if it's mutual, you are in for an irritating time, and mebbe trouble. Mebbe this is a small thing, but it's a good one to be aware of. If you happen to have quite a string tied or tailed together, sometimes these whims can raise hell. Like people, some horses hold grudges easy and stay mad for a long time. Some hold a grudge against just one particular horse. Some flare up quick and calm down quicker. Get to know your ponies as soon as you can, and watch out for the grudge-holders.

Most any good stock hand is a pretty fair roper. A few are very good. But there is lots of times you may give yourself enough rope to do your own hanging. Only the rope-happy gents use their ropes when it's good judgment to do a job another way. There are lots of good ropers who are good stock hands and fine horsemen; but there are some more rope-happy gents who are durn poor stock hands.

It's poor policy to rope a horse when you can talk him into doing right. Nobody from Point Barrow to Tierra del Fuego likes to be roped, burned, or hung. No horse or any other critter likes it any better than you do. In the corral, it's the show-off or four-flusher who ropes a horse who can be walked up to. This gent hasn't yet grown up. Bad enough in a corral; with a pack outfit a wild-eyed gent with his trusty rope may get to foul up a whole procession. So many times you get into jams that a well-handled animal can be talked out of, so you can walk up to him. When you have an animal's confidence and trust, you can usually straighten out the difficulty with no grief to anybody or anything. Lots of times you need that rope

Rope happy gent in a jam.

you've got coiled up, and need it bad, but most of the time, just leave it on the strap, it'll last longer.

Mebbe it's just their disposition, or it could be the way they were broke, but there's some horses that always seem to be snorty and kicky no matter how long you use them. It pays to keep your eyes open around them all.

Well, you're off. How far can you go in a day? I believe that fifteen miles per day through rough country, pack, unpack, pack, unpack, is plenty for any pack string, if you are on a trip that forces you to travel every day. You should carry enough oats to compensate for the continual travel. Horses and mules, and all other grass eaters that do not ruminate or chew their cud, have to get more food than those that do—such as cows, goats, camels, yaks, and so on. Grass doesn't come in cans or handy packages. The pack ponies and their cousins have to gather it. Sometimes the time is short, and sometimes so is the feed. Where camp is not moved every day, and where you have a change of horses, twenty miles or more a day isn't bad, on good feed and with layovers to rest up.

Before I end this stretch, I've a few thoughts to get down on short-tailed horses. Maybe it is fashionable to trim or pull a horse's tail short. Of course, you don't want a horse's tail to drag the ground, but you can trim a pony's pride too short for your own good and his. There is a lot about streamlining and keeping up with the well-known Joneses. Also it seems the Creator put flies, ticks, bugs of all sorts, and other prickly investigators here, to make things interesting for man and beast. The tails of various and sundry animals were evidently put on their strategic parts to irritate the fun-loving insects. You are losing money and time when you trim them too short, because their efforts to rid themselves of what they can't, causes them to run off fat, strength, and energy that you can use. Besides, if you plan to tail horses together, and find them too short, you are out of luck. So when you see a broomtail with an abbreviated fly-swatter frantically trying to get a little peace and quiet, you can see that sometimes it's painful to be fashionable.

When pack horses are turned loose to be driven, there are several ways to tie up the halter rope. Some packers try to keep a horse from feeding along the trail, so they tie the halter rope with a slip hitch high in the middle of the pack. I would rather slip the rope doubled around through the right side of the headstall of the halter, and tie a bowline around the neck, snug. He doesn't get snarled up so easy if he has to go through low-limbed trees, and maybe get snared.

103

I heard a packer once say that he had packed for forty years, but his pardner called him a blamed liar. When these characters had got done arguing, they agreed that he had packed for only twenty years, the other twenty he had spent hunting for lost horses.

So, if you want to hold your horses, and keep them safe, you'd better study on it. Just a minute, Bud. Did you bring that stock salt along?

MAKING CAMP

When a pack outfit pulls into that timber-surrounded park, horses and men are tired and hungry. No moon to shine down on frozen ropes, the frosty packs hide empty bellies. The only light that glitters is in the leering eye of that big horned owl on the limb above you. The horses are tied to trees, ready to start unpacking. Let's not have any wrecks. Don't allow any horse as much as two feet of halter rope, and tie him at least four feet off the ground. You can turn a flip-flop, or a real houlihan, in the dark on that low-tied rope. Another good way to have a wreck is to tie a pony to a small *dead* tree or limb, then let him get spooked by some packer flopping a pack cover on a nearby horse. The wind comes up and pops that tarp, your pony rares back and snaps that dead wood, and there we go again. Tie to *live* trees. And, Bud, you'd better have rivets, needle and thread, and whang leather, and also know-how, right in your war bag.

Keep an eye on those grudgeholders. Many good horses have been crippled by having a horse tied to a shallow-rooted green tree, when somebody ties a horse with a grudge against him to the same tree. Lots of times the tree gets pulled up by the roots, and there is hell to pay. A tug of war and no holds barred. Sometimes the reins or ropes break before damage is done, but usually there is hide and blood all over the scenery.

You're hungry, so's the horses. (Look out! that pack horse just tried to lie down and roll.) You've got to unpack, bell and hobble the horses and turn 'em loose, picket a couple of wrangle horses; and you got to help the cook or do it yourself.

I hope you got in mind which horse you are using to carry the panniers or packs that contain your kitchen outfit, food, and all the things you need to start a meal with. Hope you put in last the things you are going to need first. Mumble and fumble, what horse is this? Ain't he the one with the grub? Jerk this, pull that, oh man, *then* it pays to know your own knots and hitches! The cook is in a hurry, unpack that kitchen outfit first, then the food; the tents and beds and the rest of the gear, last.

As each animal is unpacked, he is led off and tied. His pack saddle, with his name on it, is taken off. Stack pack saddle, pads, and blanket near

Tug of war, and no holds barred.

where you're going to pitch the gear tent, with pad and blanket on top of saddle, spread flat to air out and dry; lash and sling rope on top, pack cover over all.

Many packers pitch a tent in which to store pack saddles, blankets, pads, oats, rope, and odds and ends of supply. A small tent weighs little, and is a labor-saving protection. Wet and frozen sling and pack rope is the meanest thing to handle there is. When it's wet, it's shrunk. When it dries out, it stretches, and your packs loosen up. Rock chucks and porcupines love rope, salty, sweat-soaked leather, and a lot more of your plunder. So use a tent for all your saddles, pads, rope, shoeing outfit, tools, oats, and all your extra horse gear. They stay dry, and are usually protected from marauding animals, including pet horses.

If you don't have a gear tent, a good deal is to lash a big 20-foot pole four feet off the ground from tree to tree. Trim it clean, and stack your saddles along its length. Coil your rope gear on top, then lay your pads and blankets flat, cover with pack covers and manties. (See Plate 2.) With this deal, stack your oats with your food, in the cook tent.

Handle your horses your own way: but a good time-, trouble-, and horse-saving deal is to take care of the horse proposition *right after* their loads

are taken off. When people in a country strange to them unpack their outfit, dilly-dally around till dark, then put their horse bunch in a big moose
swamp with willowy bogs, rocky trap holes, and snaggy beaver house vil-
lages, they are in for bellyaches and scattered horses. It's so plumb dark
by then that they tie their picket horses to snaggy logs in some little tangled
park full of blowdowns, and then stumble back to camp.

If you can locate your horse bunch on good feed, and picket or stake
your wrangle horses in safe places before dark, right after unpacking, you
can sleep easy and get up late. Why walk when you can ride?

Startling disclosures are sometimes the result of tieing up in the wrong
place. I once saw a young gent, sort of damp behind his two hearing aids,
tie up a horse to a small tent rope. Something inside jiggled the tent and
spooked this noble friend of man. Away went horse, with tent, stove-pipe,
half a bed roll, and clothes hung up on a rope inside. There stood a nude
old dude, startled and mad. He was taking a wash from a water pail. We
caught and calmed the horse, but the kid was so spooky that we figured on
picketing him by the foot until the old man soothed down.

Keep a clean camp as you go along; then, when you pack out, bury your
cans, clean up all the debris, and stack your poles. There's bears, forest
rangers, and other people around.

I know of some places in the California mountains (and perhaps there
may be more) where, over the years, so many people have packed into the
hills, that Patino, the tin king of South America, would get the grasping
d.t.s. The places to bury the empties are plumb exhausted. The shovel,
trying to dig a hole, is blunted by more metal than the mountains can take.
In this case, the way to keep the country like God made it, is to pound the
cans flat, load 'em in your empty panniers, and pack them back down to
some town dump to be bulldozed, for the future archeologists to puzzle over
in centuries to come. They don't weigh much, and it's little work to keep
the country clean.

GETTING ALONG WITH THE WILDERNESS

If you can't pack it out, don't kill it. There's an old saying that will live forever, "Discretion is the better part of valor." Mebbe you will think of it after you kill that fine bull elk in the canyon jungle. Hunting's been tough, it's late in the season, and that slate-colored sky has been spitting snow all day long. Colder than it was yesterday. Only four hours ago you heard a bull bugle; then there was some running, some clattery, branch-breaking thumps, in the steep, rocky timber high above you. Now you've dressed him out, couldn't hardly roll him over and up on pieces of log, so he'll be off the ground and not sour. Biggest bull you ever seen. You finally put your knife back in the scabbard, and sit down, out of the wind coming down the canyon. You roll a smoke, lean against an enormous boulder, and think, Boy, I'm all set now.

You look down at the faint silvery ribbon of a creek, twisting along far below those cliffs that are just below you and your bull. In the gathering darkness, you gaze up above you, at the steep and rough, rock-strewn, timbered mountain, and wonder how any elk or human could ever have come down through that steep jungle of rocks and heavy timber, crisscrossed with deadfalls and blowdowns. The worst jungle in the Rockies. About then you wonder how you're going to pack mebbe 400 pounds of elk out of there. Only one way, and durn near straight up. Five miles to the tepee and the old pickup. No mules, no horses. Probably couldn't get a pack animal through that mess if you had one, let alone take a load out. That's when you make the New Year's resolution you're going to keep—I'll let him live unless I need him *and* can get him out and use him.

Did you never sit on a log in open timber waiting for some live winter meat to show up? Eat your lunch and have a camp-robber fly by and cafeteria a piece of your sandwich? If not, you don't know his sharing ideas, but he takes his opportunities to show you.

Sure, I don't like a porcupine in my tent to wake me up at night. His social graces and etiquette wasn't gotten from Emily Post. He has had his own manners, before ever the human had any himself. Only the porcupine's manners are steadfast—he doesn't follow fashion's whims or fancies.

108

If you can't pack it out, don't kill it.

I'm not back home now; I'm in Rome, and I'd best follow the Roman manners.

If you follow the etiquette of the new country, obey and respect the laws and customs of the land, the inhabitants will welcome you, and maybe want to be friendlier than your civilized heart can bear. There are four-footed peddlers and salesmen galore, but their wares are mostly profit-sharing in a different sense than ours; and there are ways to discourage them and still be friends. We may really be getting away from it all when we hit the hills. We are in a different life, all right. Something is always going on. The sheriff, the police, and the law as the settlements know it, is gone. It's a different law out with our mountain and plains native inhabitants. Their law is survival, though with it you'll encounter pride, humor, and curiosity. Some of them try to put by for winter and old age. They got no pensions or social security. The only taxes they pay are sometimes fatal, and paid to the human who invades their domain. They like respect, understanding, appreciation, and a little tolerance, same as our kids down in the valleys below. They are willing to share what they have, and feel that one good turn deserves another, even if our system of measurement isn't always the same one they go by.

What do you expect, anyhow? Yeah, you left your creel full of them big cutthroats lay on the bank while you went over to that pot hole under them spruce to try for another big one. Sure, you couldn't carry it because you might over-balance into the canyon. Shoulda hung it on a branch. That big ol' mink thought they was bananas, so he sampled each one. Different flavor in each fish, I think!

I thought the guy knew enough to leave a coat or a slicker by his game. That big ol' black bear sure did chaw up a hind quarter of his bull moose he was so proud of. When we went to pack it down this morning, that old bear was just starting in on one of the fronts. Naw, Tom didn't even nick him with that old Krag—too excited, I guess.

Most hunters know about magpies, ravens, and crows; they've heard about the hunter who spent three days helping his friends before he went back to pack his elk in—the birds left him just a skeleton. It's against the law, even!

Next time we *all* go fishing we sure want to tie up all our tent flaps. Means nobody home, and most animals respect that—well, most of the big polite ones, anyhow. I'll admit, though, some bear like to make their own openings!

110

You know the reason the cook was grumpy this morning? Oh, boy, wait till I tell his wife down to the ranch! About one o'clock this morning a couple of snowshoe rabbits decided to cross his bed in order to get a bite or two of oats. (He'd stacked a couple extra sacks in the back end of his cook tent.) They tried three or four times. At first, Shorty thought a couple young moose were in there with him. When he woke up in that old tarp bed of his and looked into the frosty moon, it was the perspective, plus the hard thumps of those eight big feet on his corns, that caused that helluva yell we heard. Naw, that wasn't no mountain lion, that was the cook! He says he's going to close his tent flaps tonight. He thought he was going to get away from it all, but he says now it's quieter down to the ranch.

"Are you a man or a mouse?" is a saying that makes you look at the chipmunks over in that hard pannier we put the biscuits in. Sure, it's *our* tent and *our* camp. That's right, that big mule deer and her spotted fawn were stealing licks from the horses' block of salt last night, too. Yeah, and I seen them white-footed mice stealing oats in the gear tent. I also heard a pack rat jingling the rowels on Slim's spurs last night. The only reason he couldn't add them to his antique collection was that Slim always leaves them strapped to his boots.

Sure, Slim got mad when he found his new throw rope chawed right in two in the middle by that dang nosy rockchuck. Slim is a pretty good rope splicer, though, and did you hear him bawl out the horse wrangler for trying to shoot a rockchuck? Well!

The only reason your bridle and headstall was chewed on was you throwed your gear on the ground and didn't protect it.

Hell, yes, I was hungry, too, but I still think it's funny: the cook forgot to tie the tent flap strings, and that dang pet pinto camp horse knocked over the dutch oven when he moseyed into the cook tent. He sure ate all them cold baked trout. Damn Swede horse.

In camp and on the trail we're among Romans who have got but very little to get along with, but mebbe they get along as well as we do at home. Ordinarily, to eat when you're hungry, to drink when you're dry, to sleep when you're tired and sleepy—those things, plus to clean up when you're dirty, to be warm when it's cold, to be cool when it's hot, and to be healthy, are all our essential needs. These things are fundamental, rich or poor, all races, creeds, and colors; and also whether two- or four-legged, or whether wearing hair, fur, or feathers.

111

Well, we humans have got a corner, mebbe, on ambition: drive, if you want to call it that. Competition and rivalry makes for progress, so it is said—keeping up with the Joneses mebbe is a byproduct. Say and think what you will, atomic or plastic, this fact still remains: when you die, you are dead, and no mistake!

There's another old one, "Men may come, and men may go, but I go on forever." When you tarry by that sunny, shadowy, rushing, cool, sweet mountain stream, you've gotten away from it all. It don't take much to keep you happy.

There is a mouse (I haven't caught him yet) who's been living in the upholstery of my pickup for a long time. I don't know how long he or she has been there, but that mouse sure has been over a lot of this country and some of Canada. I'll get him yet, but I've a lot of admiration for this cuss. He takes things coming and going, and makes himself at home. His food and drink supply problem must be monumental, and sure as hell is mobile. But I'll be like Slim, I think I'll cuss around and ignore him. He's making a living somehow. In his modern choice of ways, he must have some stone age knowledge and know-how, to provide the necessities, because he's already got a fancy camp.

THIS IS THE END

Well, maybe a mouse *hasn't* got too much to do with a yarn like this. Still, a mouse, like a human, has transportation problems; as have a lot of yet smaller animals. We will all admit that a human has bigger and more complex problems to go with his larger body. Mice and humans both use pack outfits; but while mice use them as a means of migration with food supply furnished enroute, they let somebody else figure out the ways and means of transportation.

So, if you need to transport other things besides mice on pack animals, the slings and various other ties and hitches I have talked about and pictured here may help you. These methods of fastening loads to a pack saddle I have used for years in rough, timbered mountain country. They are generally in use by packers, and most of them are as old as the hills. There are other ways, and other adaptations, but the principle is the same. Whether you have been a packer for fifty years or for one year, the horse is still built the same, and so is the man. The hills have eroded a little, but are just as steep; the rocks are as hard, the water as wet, the snow as cold, and most problems encountered by a packer and guide in a rough, isolated country are the same as if you'd packed in the days of 100 years ago. You may have better materials to use in the rigs you now have, but the horse is still the horse of yesterday, and you are your own grandpa.

So long, pardner. Take it easy. Good luck.

And when you come to the end of your rope—*Tie a knot in it and hang on.*

So Long · Pardner · Take It Easy ·
Good Luck · And When You
Come To The End Of Your Rope,

TIE A KNOT IN IT,

AND HANG ON!

APPENDIX   A list that was used and worked out OK.

Food and equipment—5 persons—16 days

FOOD
5-lb can jam
side of bacon
6 doz. eggs
1 ham
4 lb frankfurters
5 steaks (first evening)
6 cans pork & beans
6 cans spaghetti-meat balls
4 cans corned beef, etc.
16 cans assorted soups
5 lb onions
5 lb turnips
1 big box Quaker Oats
2 boxes wheatena
10 lb cornmeal
25 lb potatoes
50 lb flour
20 lb sugar
1 lb salt
1 can baking powder
1 box soda
10 envelopes dry yeast
2 bunches carrots
4 cans peas, beans, corn, toms
1 jar salad dressing
4 heads lettuce
2 doz. oranges
4 cans oranges-grapefruit
6 tall cans tomato juice
6 tall cans orange juice
4 tall cans grape juice
4 pkg kraft dinner
2 lb cheese
4 lb rice
12 tall cans milk
1 case Borden's Starlac
2 bottles ketchup
pepper, vanilla, mapleine
Accent-garlic salt

4 lb butter
1 can syrup
5 lb raisins and prunes
4 pkg cookies
8 lb coffee
small pkg tea bags
4 lb cocoa
4 cans fruit cocktail
10 lb apples
6 loaves bread
1 box candy bars
5 lb p-nut butter
1 jar mustard
4 boxes dry cereal
1 can pumpkin
cinnamon-cloves-ginger
pickles
dog food
1 box crackers
4 cabbage heads

EQUIPMENT—KITCHEN
3 frying pans
3 big spoons
butcher knife
paring knife
clothespins
6 ea. knives-forks-spoons
breadboard
bug-bomb
oilcloth
lunch sacks
waxed paper
can opener
4 dish soap
2 hand soap
6 dish towels
tooth-picks
pencils
egg beater

116

napkins
toilet paper
caddy of matches
kleenex
measuring cup and spoon
strainer
dripping pan
3 lids
saucepan
kettle
large kettle
coffee pot
2 SOS, 1 can Bab-O
8 plates and cups
dish pan
wash basin

EQUIPMENT—CAMP
horseshoeing outfit
pliers
spikes
4 bells
hobbles
halters
ropes
pads
pack saddles
panniers
pack covers
5 sets saddle gear
saw file

axe file
hack saw blades
coleman lantern
    mantles
    coleman generator
    gasoline
candles
ditty-bag (buckskin, needles,
    beeswax, thread, buttons,
    scissors)
2 tepees
cook tent and fly
wire and nails
maps
first aid kit
pocket knives
fishing gear
slickers
cotton gloves
leather gloves
flashlights, batteries
note book
sleeping bags, with liners,
    mattresses
2 axes
shovel
log saw
stove
hammer
stock salt
oats

Joe Back was born in Ohio in 1899 and moved to Wyoming when he was thirteen. He served as a machine gun instructor during World War I, then took up trade as a cowboy, guide, and packer. Later he spent four years at the Art Institute of Chicago where, to use Joe's words, he "damn near starved to death." Art education changed his life, however, and although he went back to packing and guiding, he also became nationally known as a sculptor. Joe Back died September 7, 1986 at age 87—through the magic of his illustrations and writing we celebrate and share his work.